# *Footy shorts*

## FUN LITTLE CARTOONS

Printed in the United States of America

# A bit of art for the everyday bloke

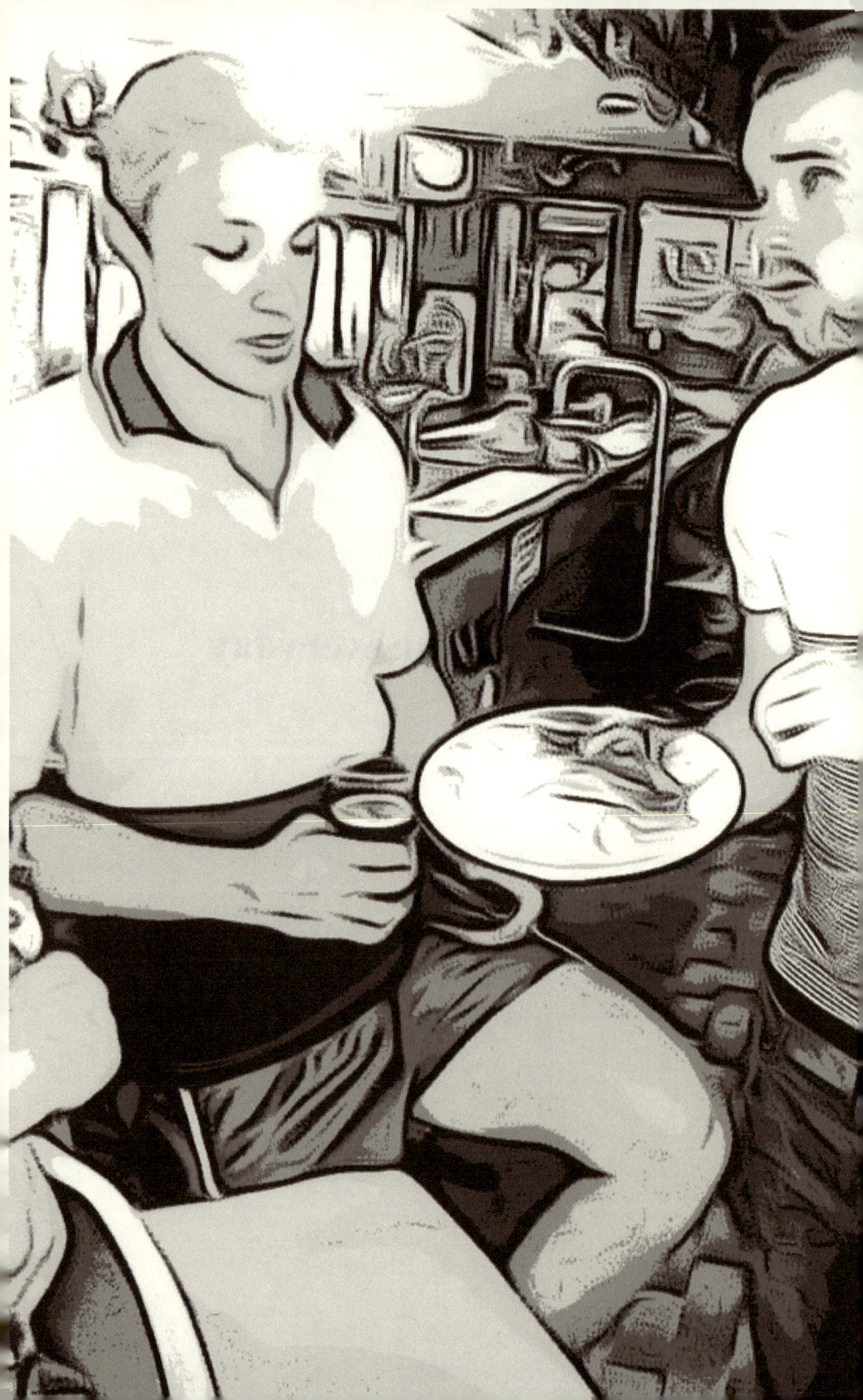

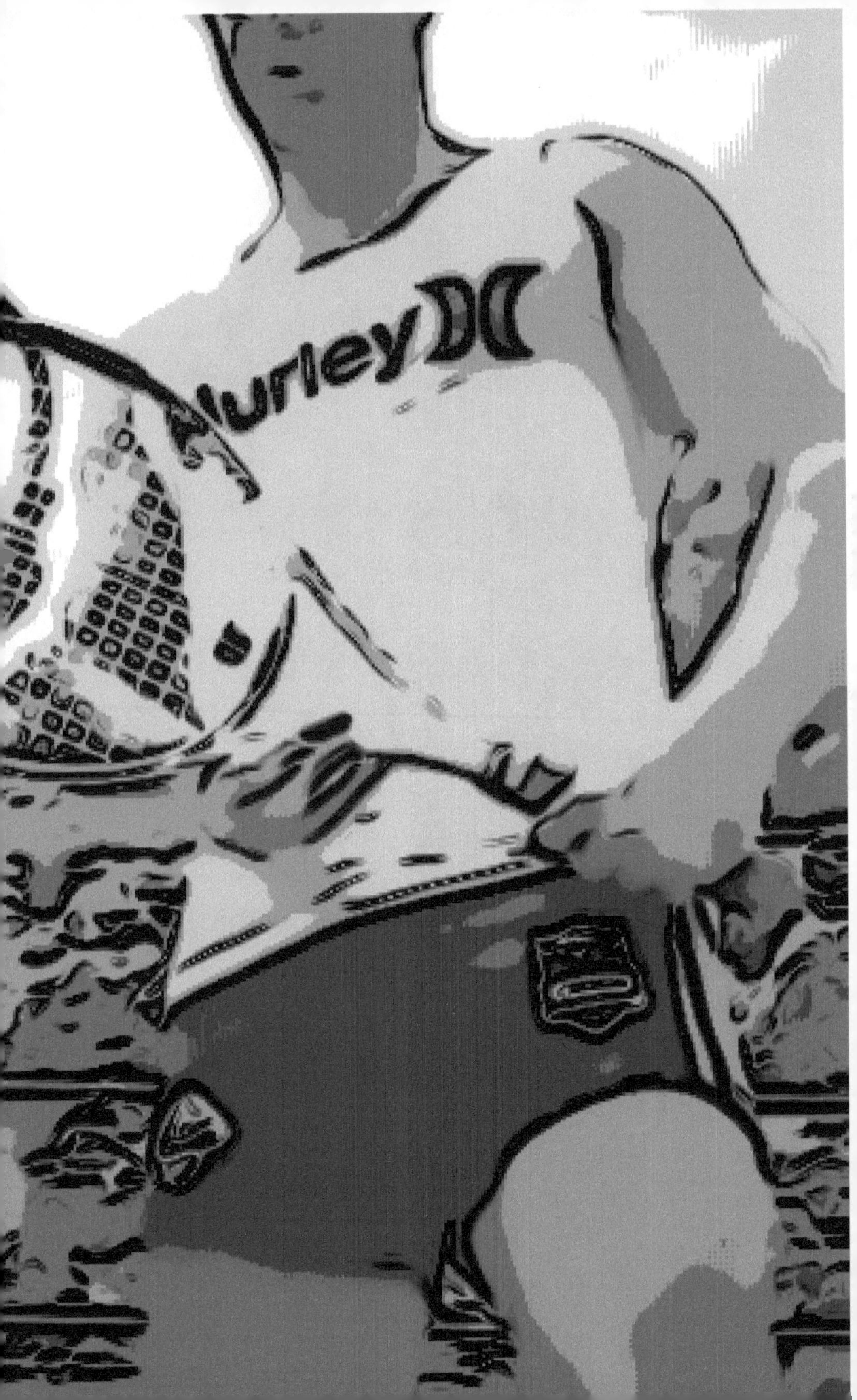

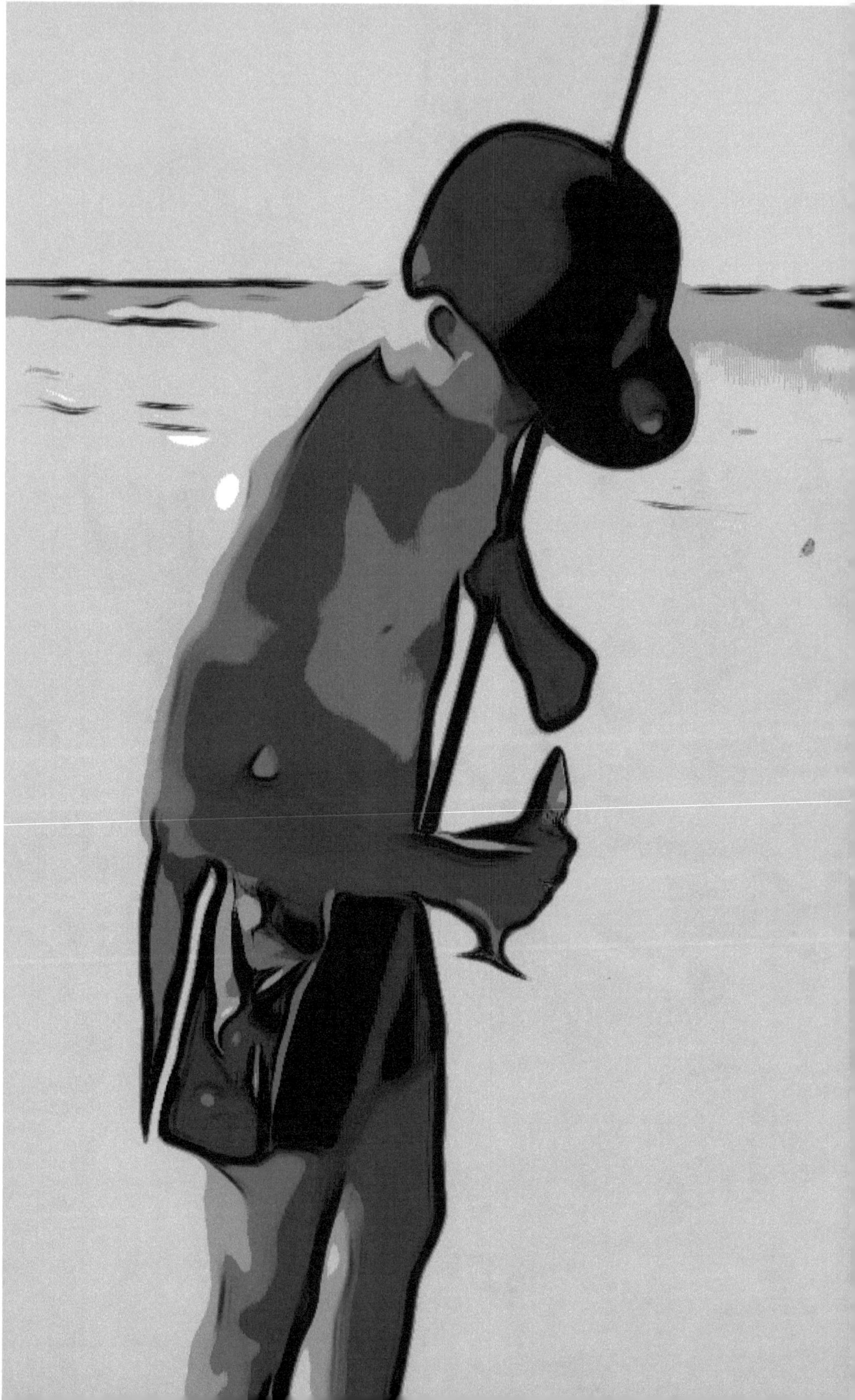

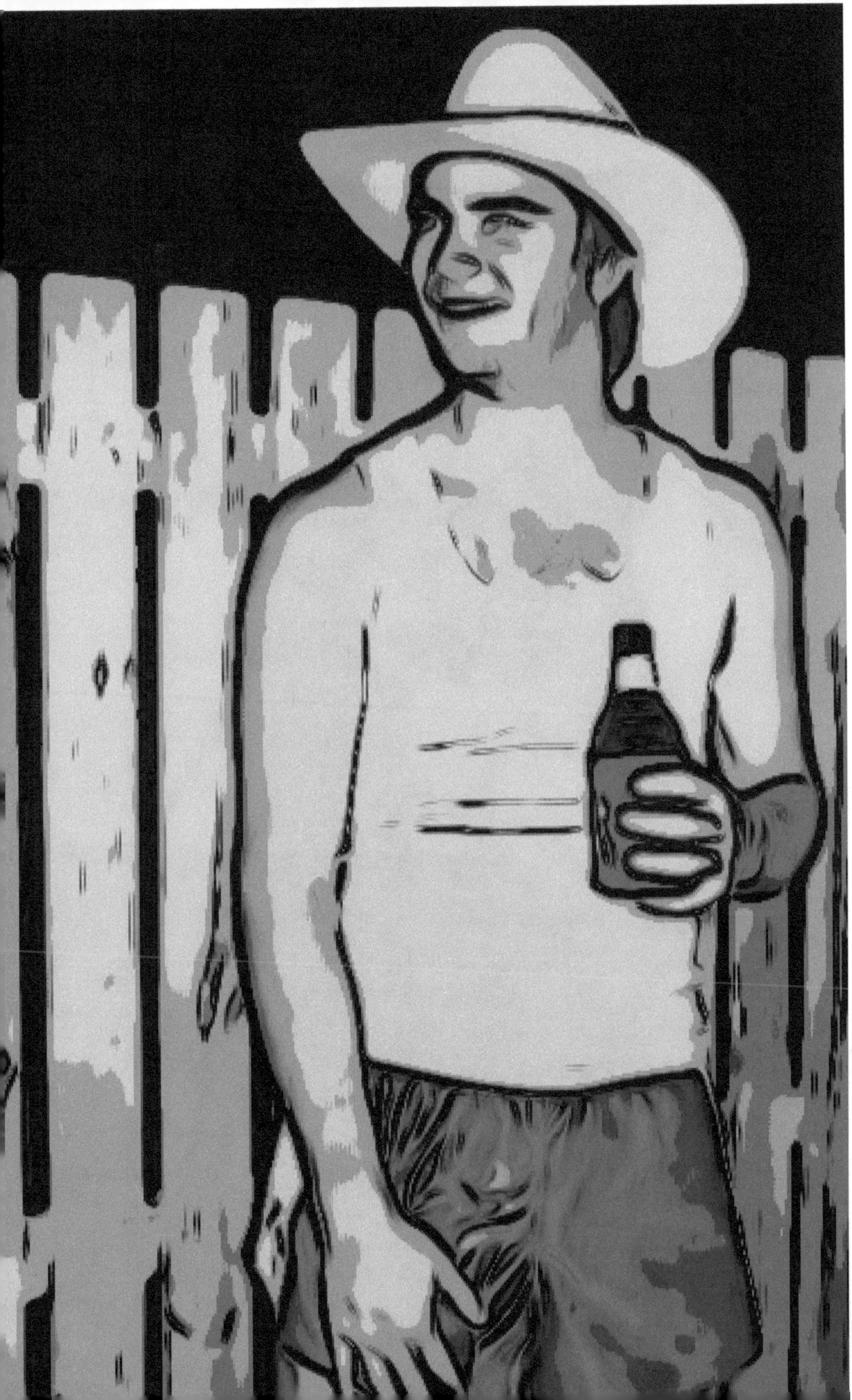

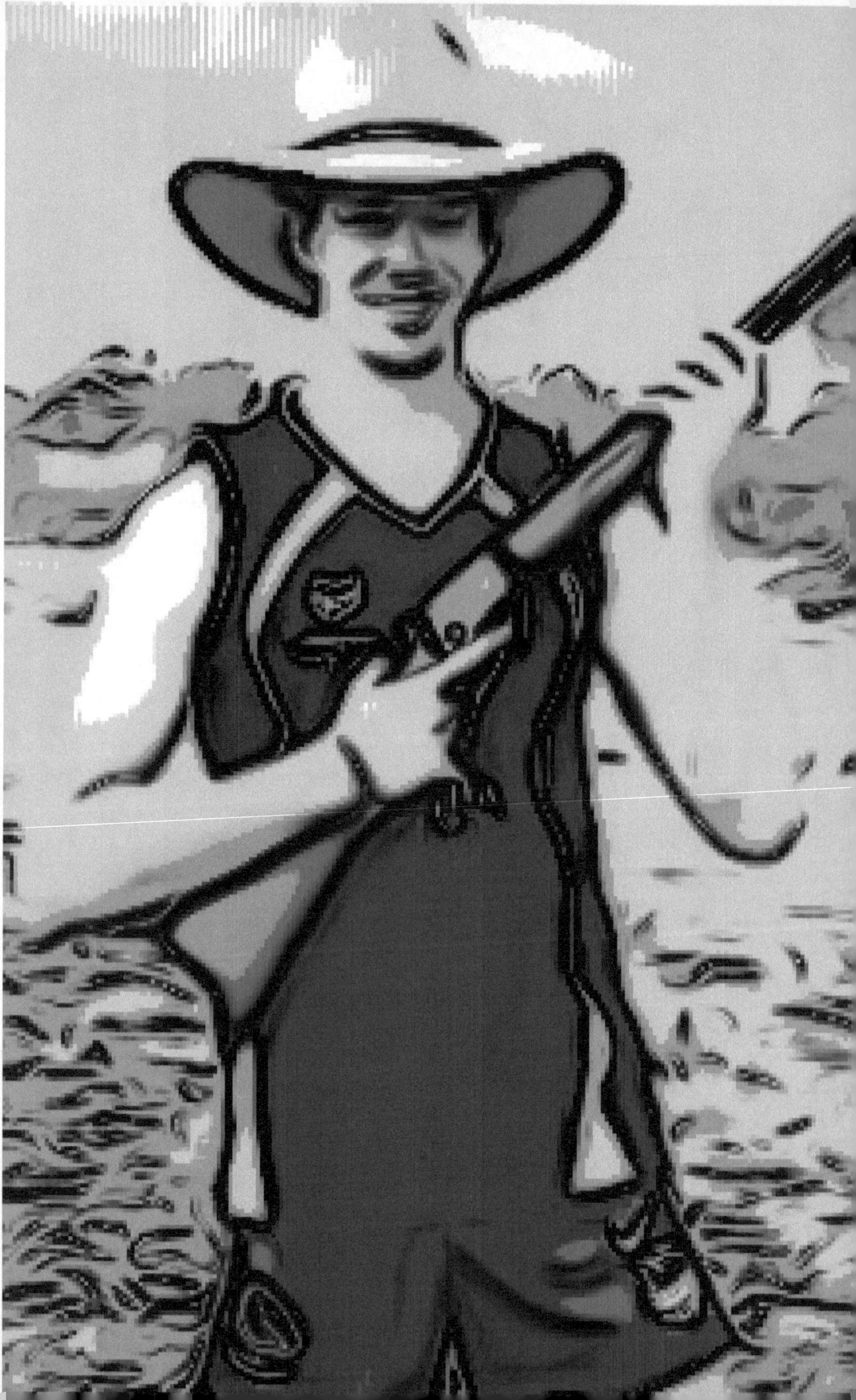

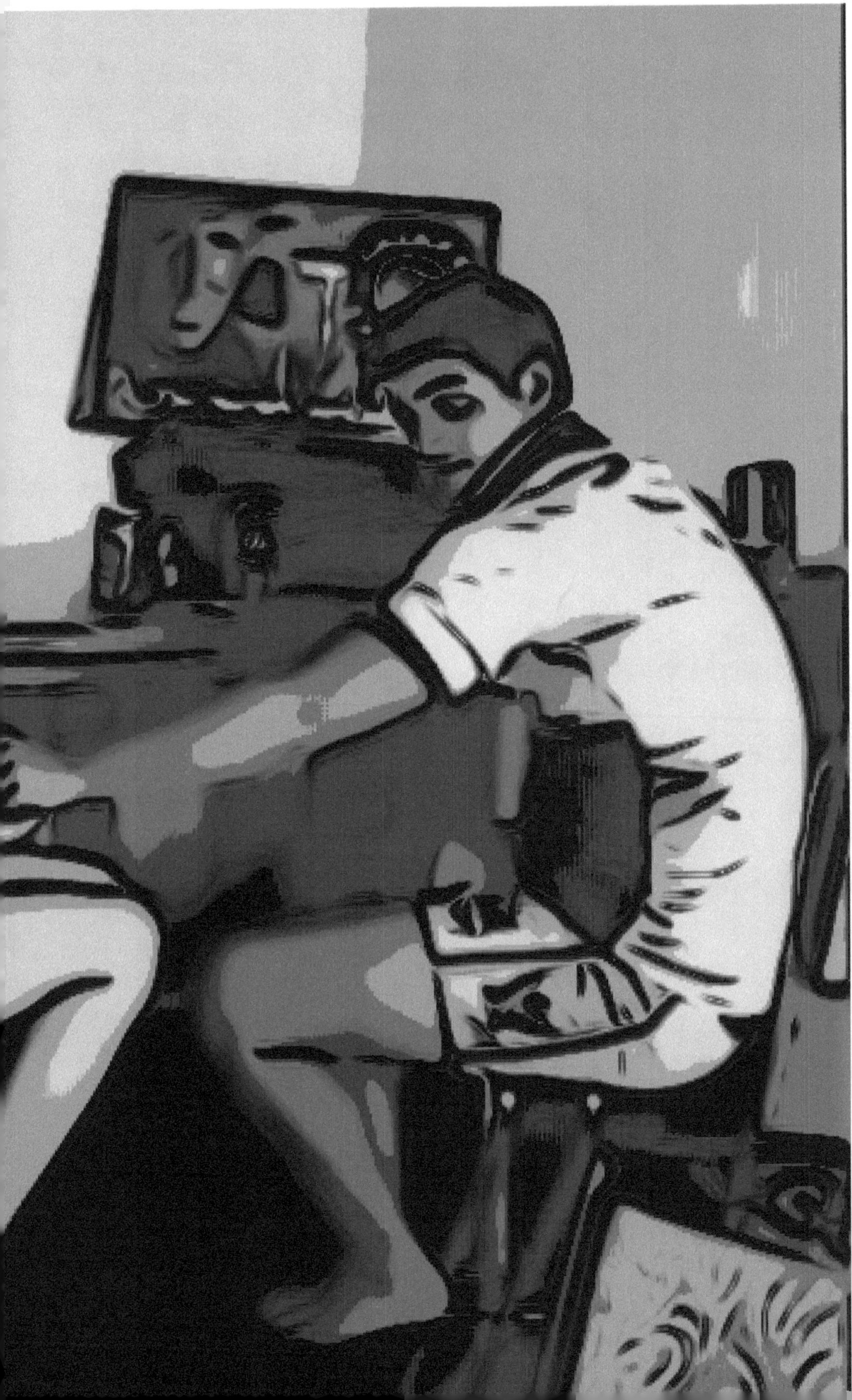

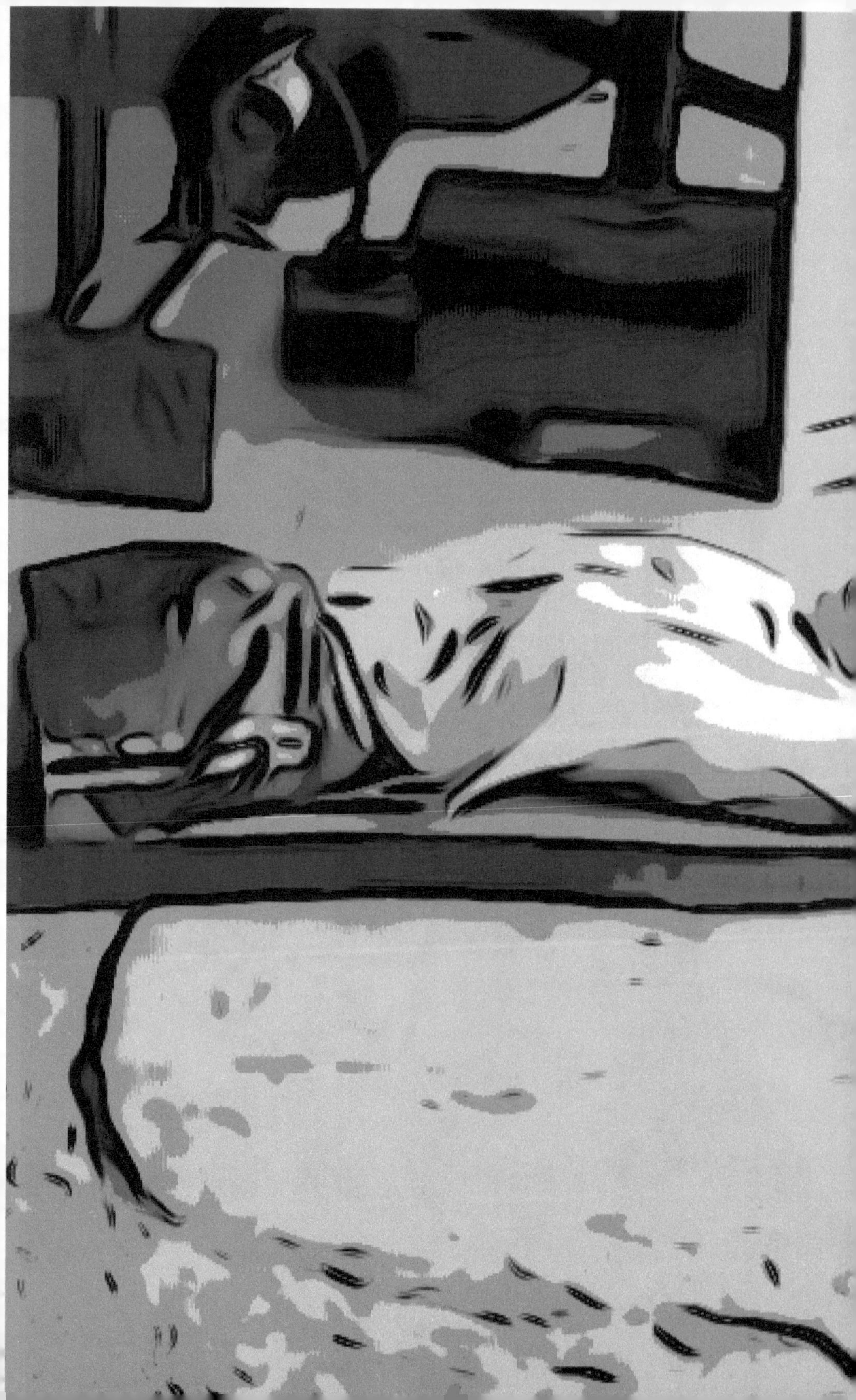

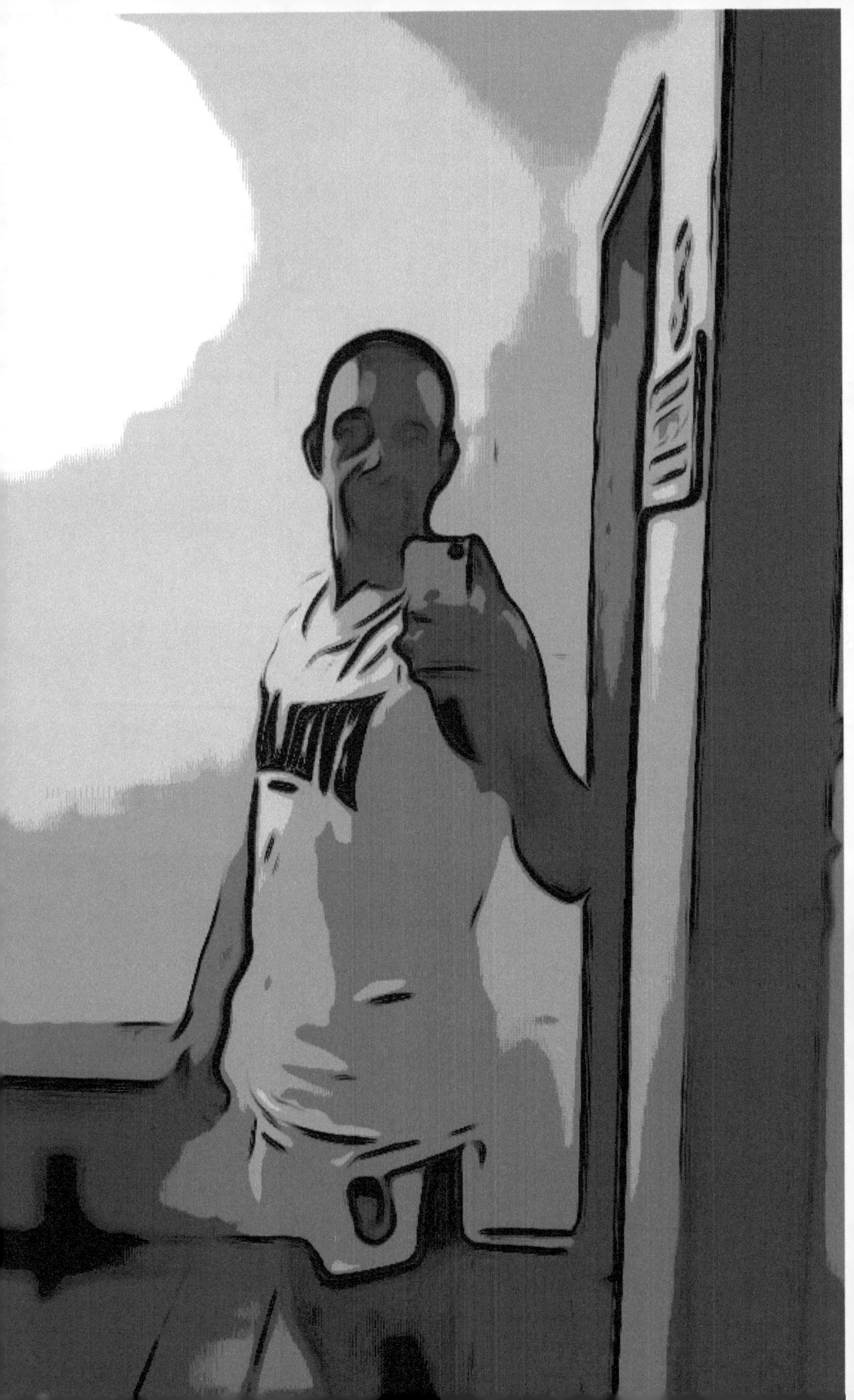

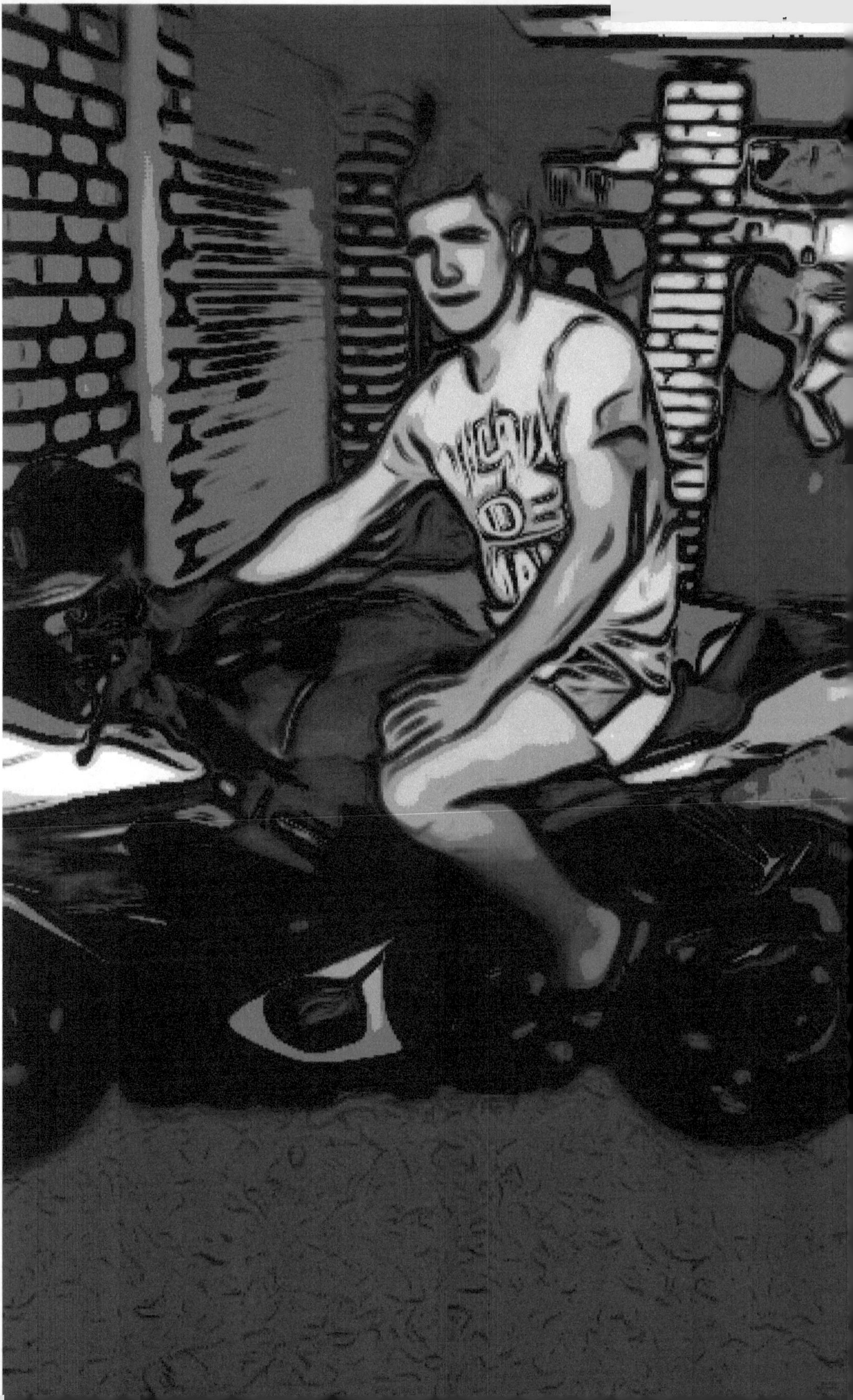

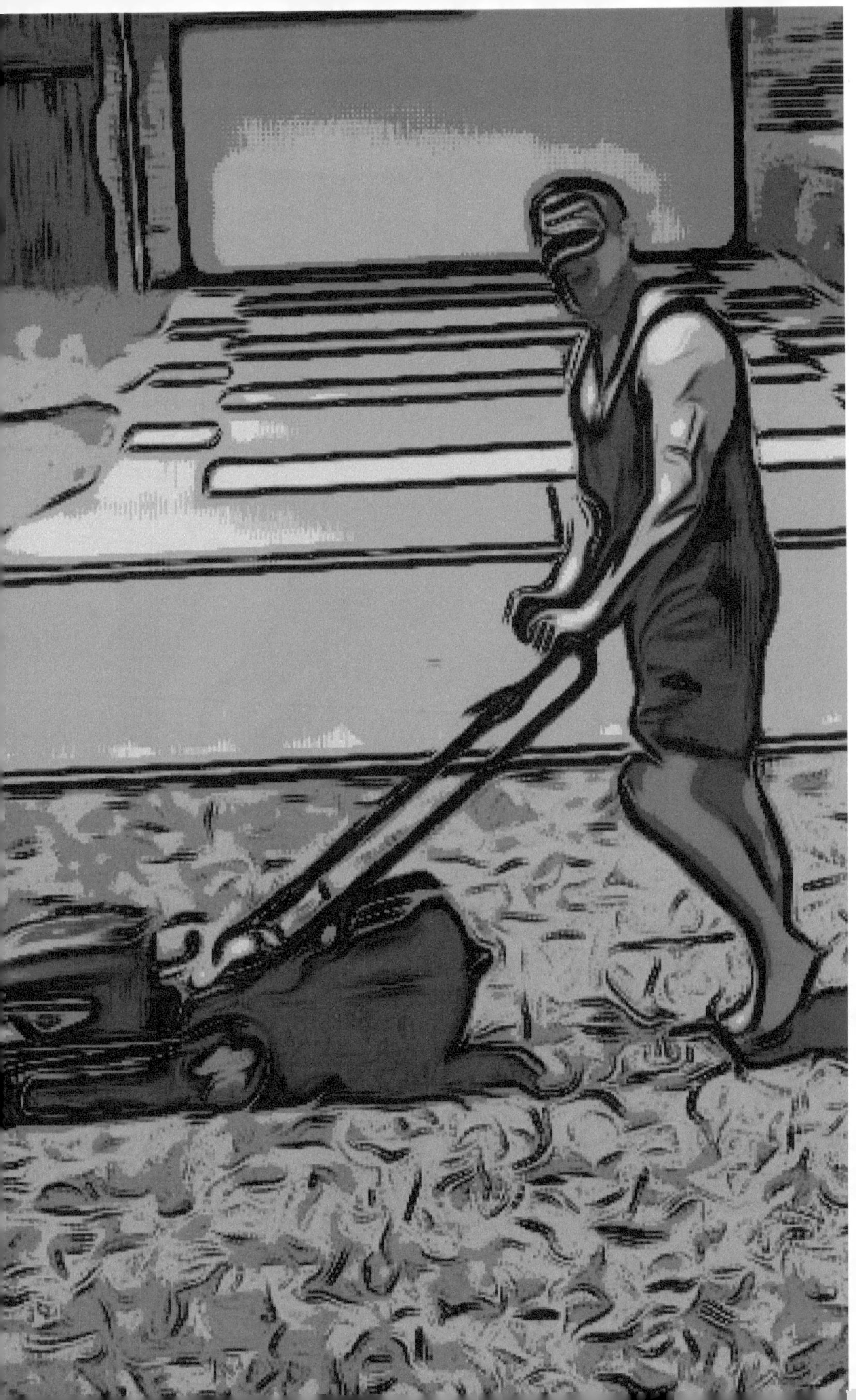

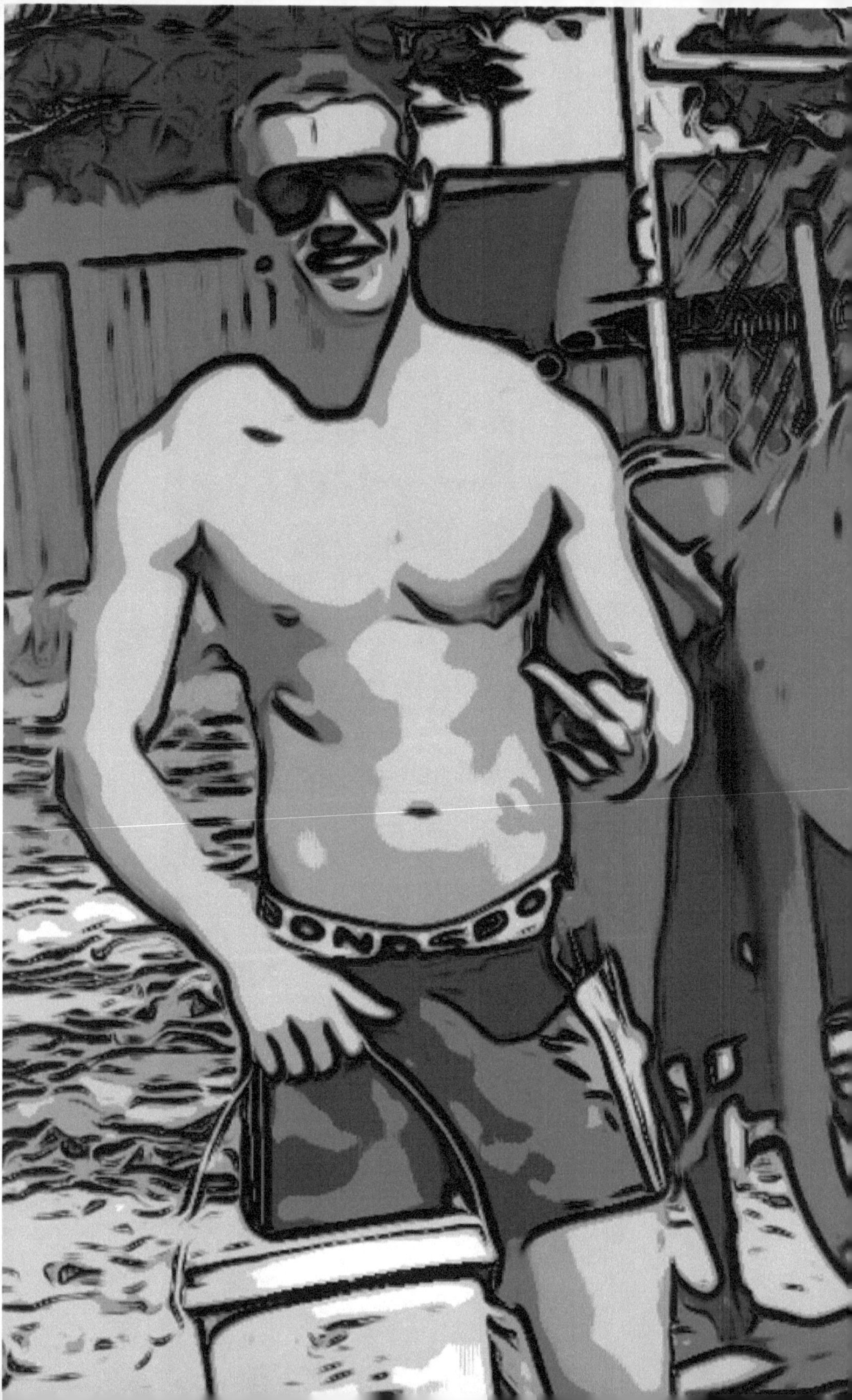

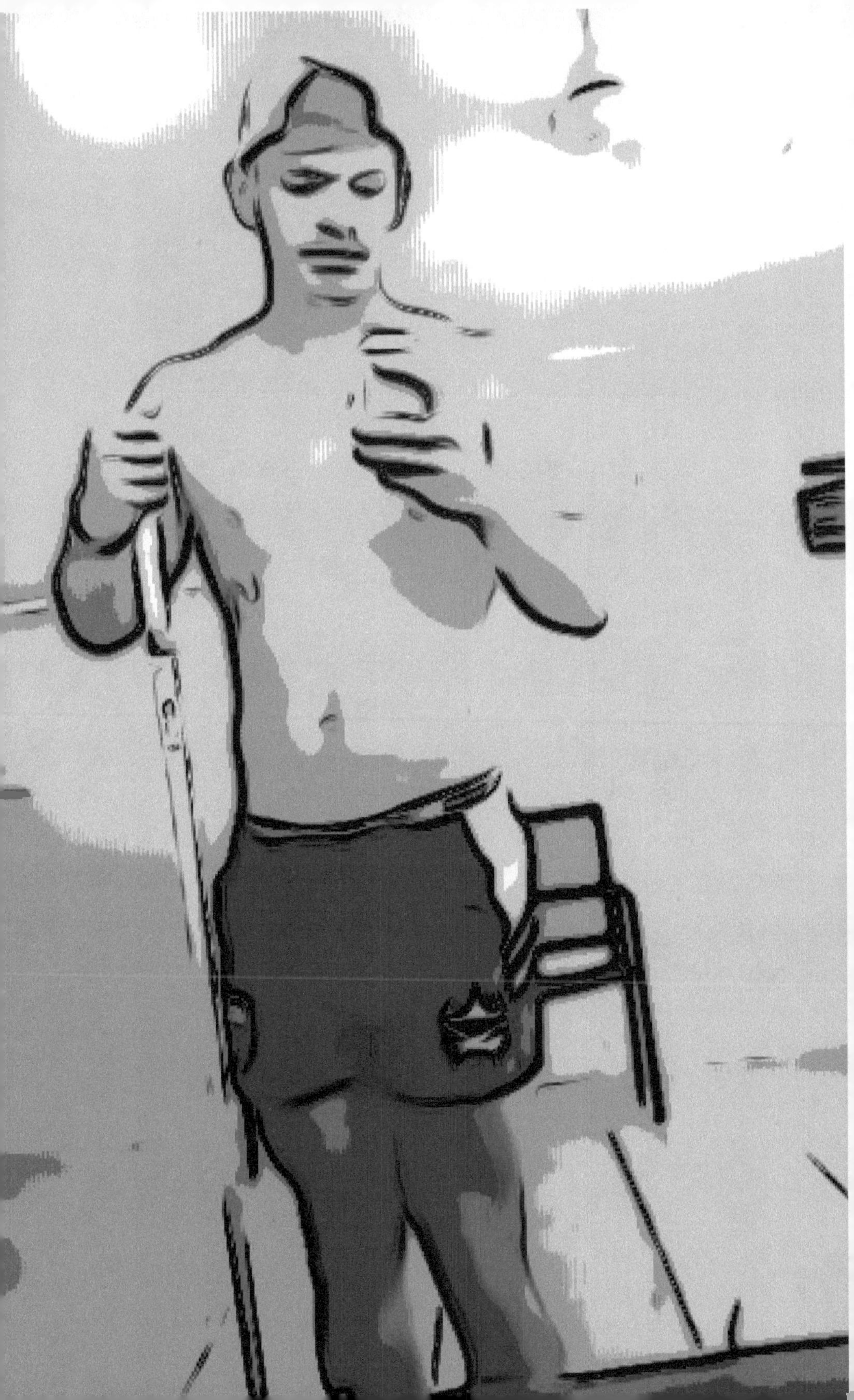

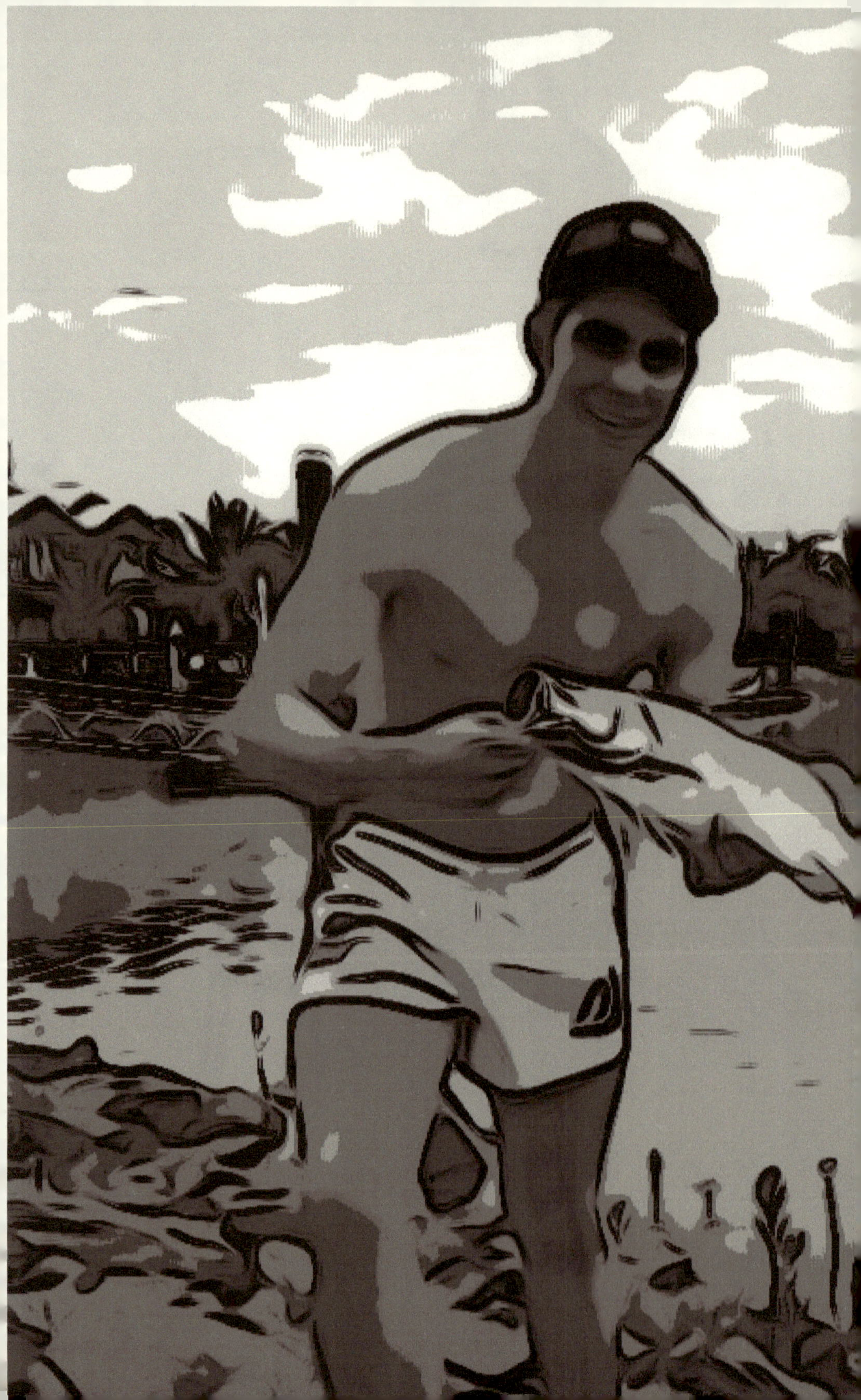

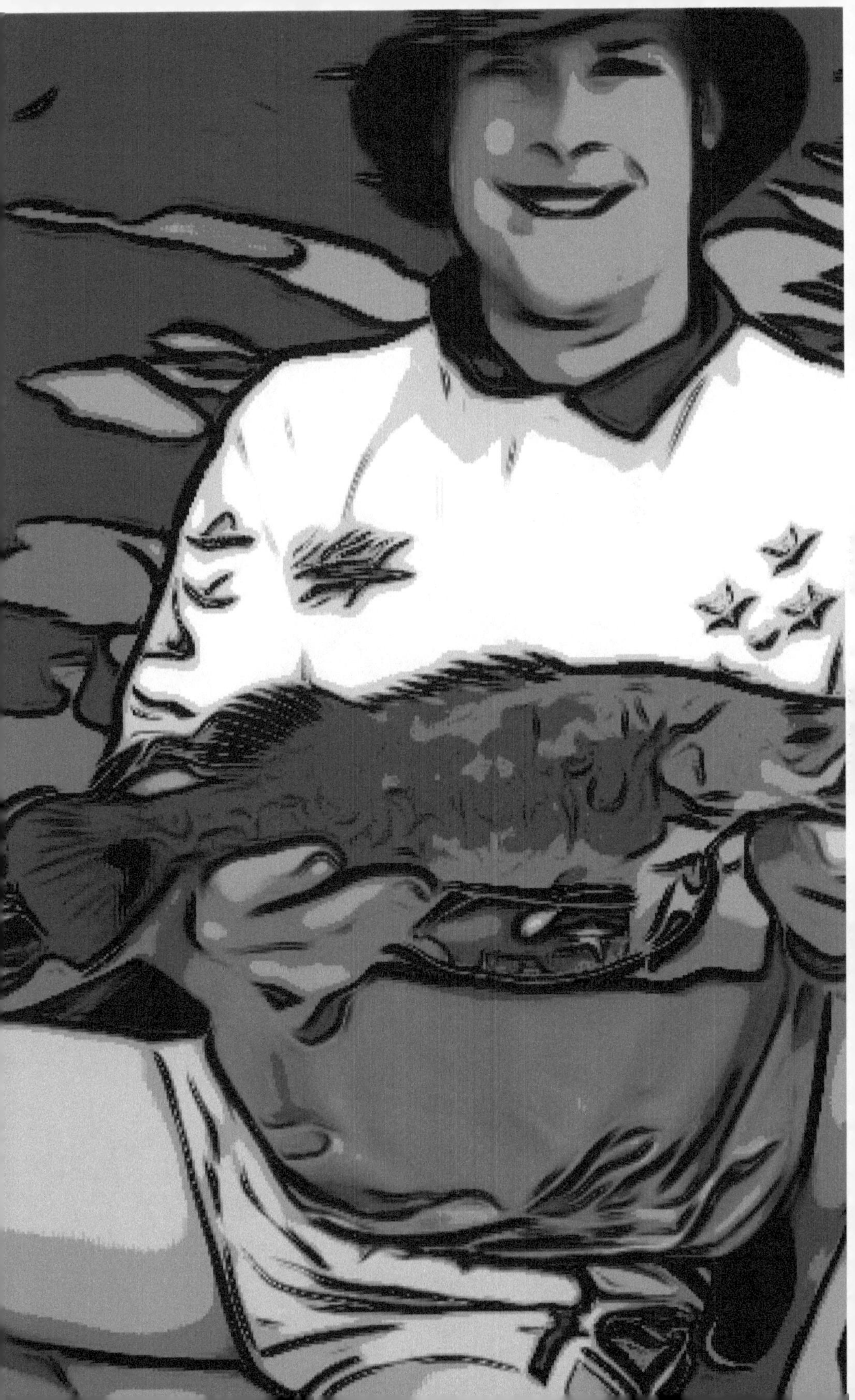

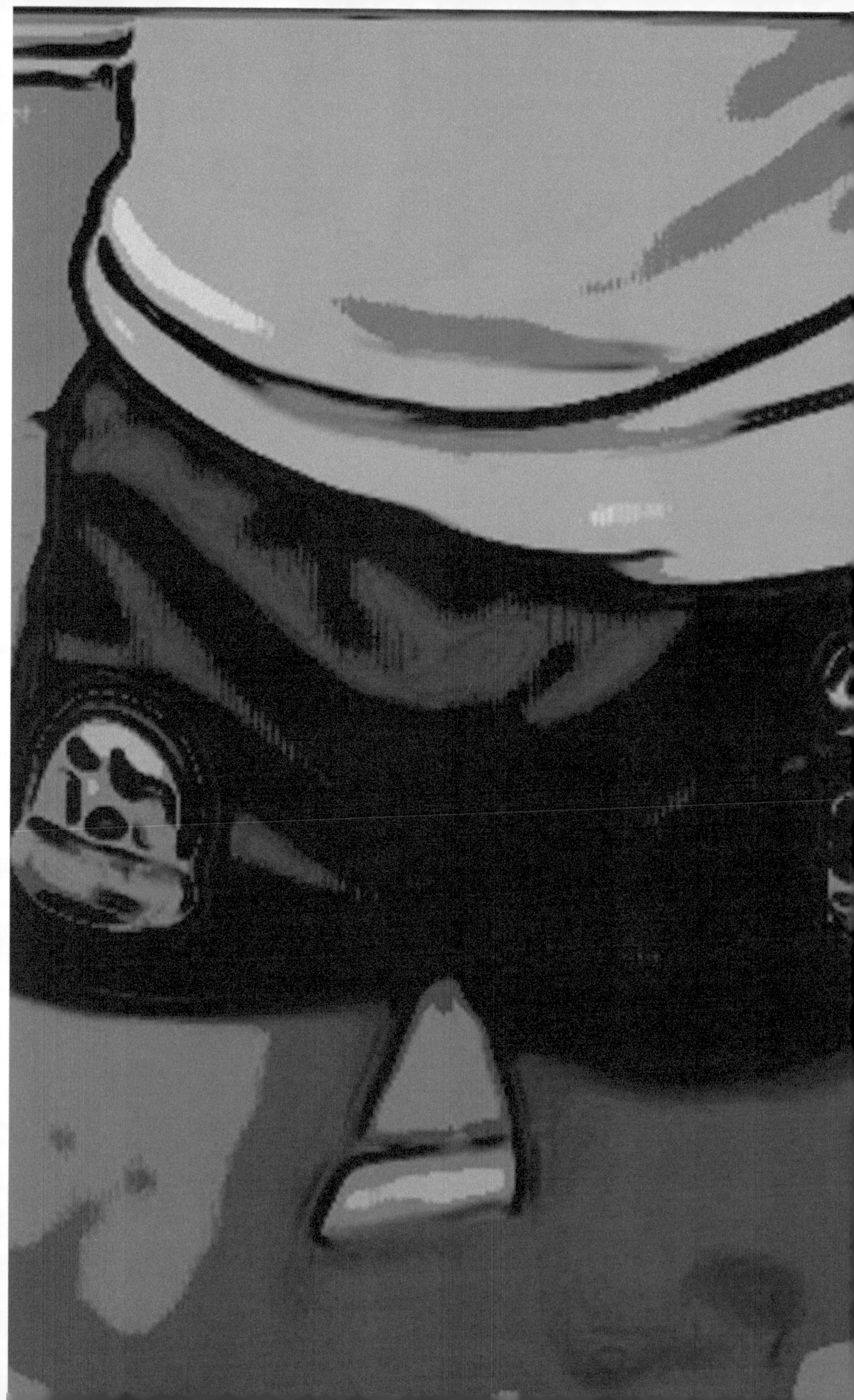

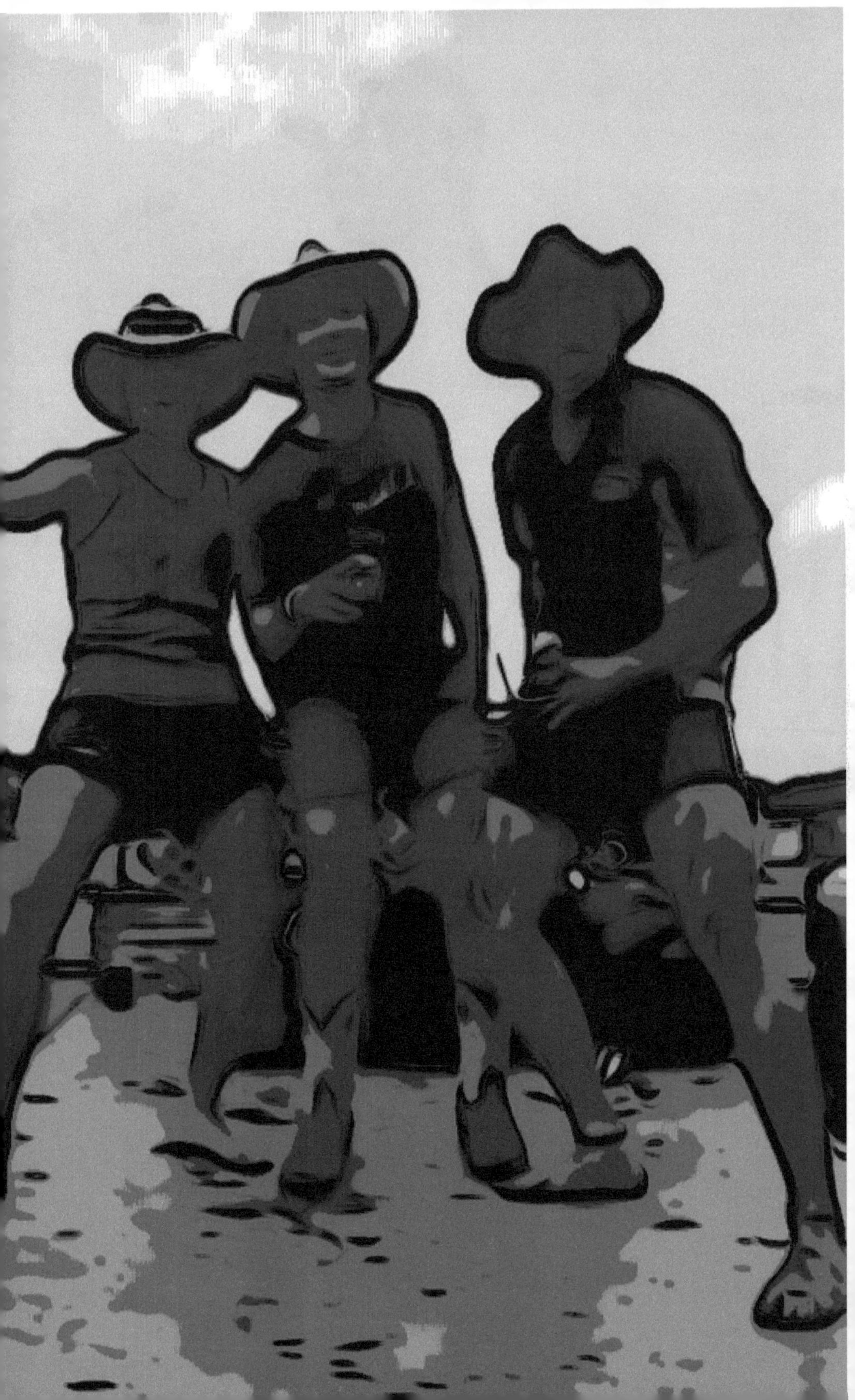

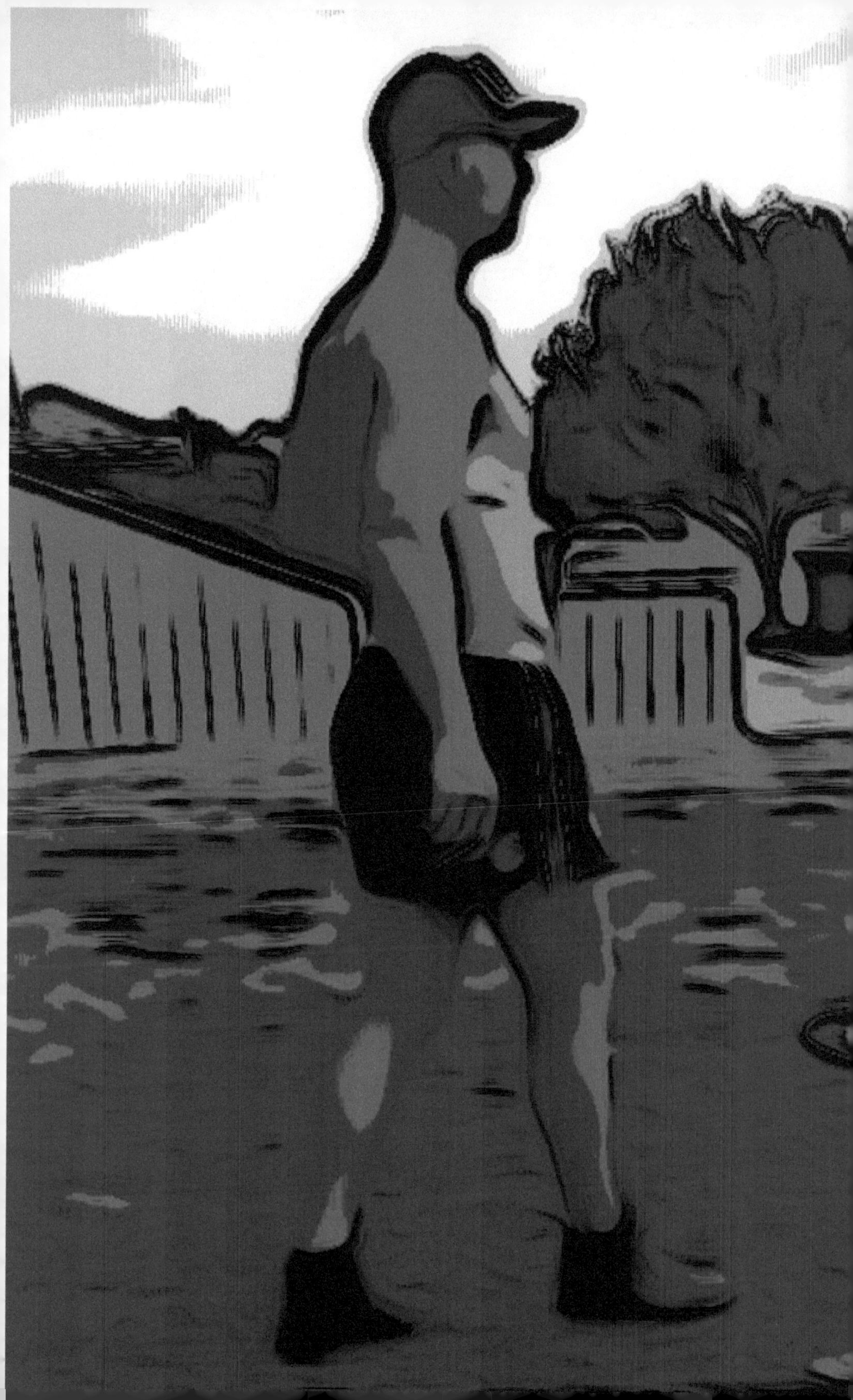

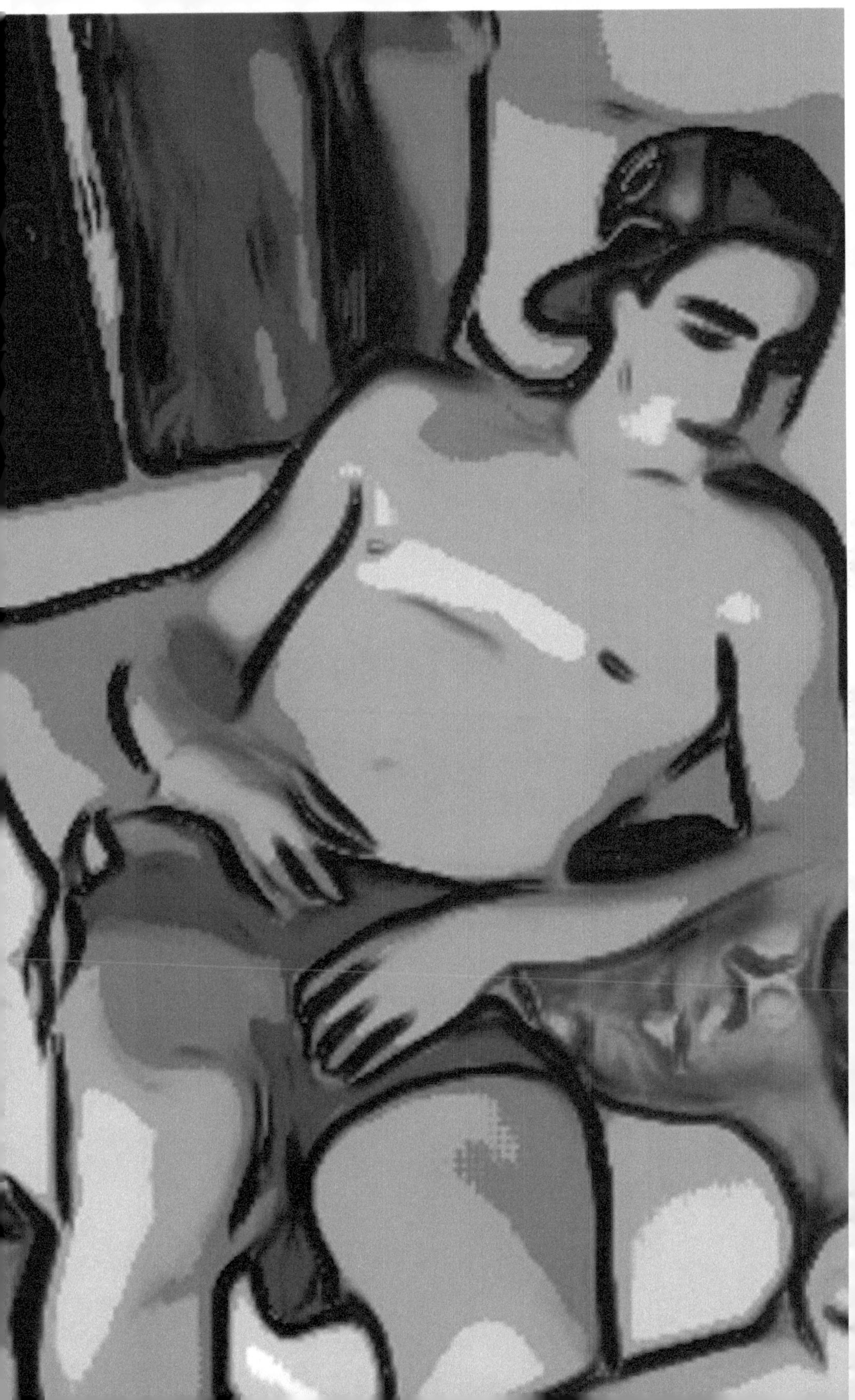

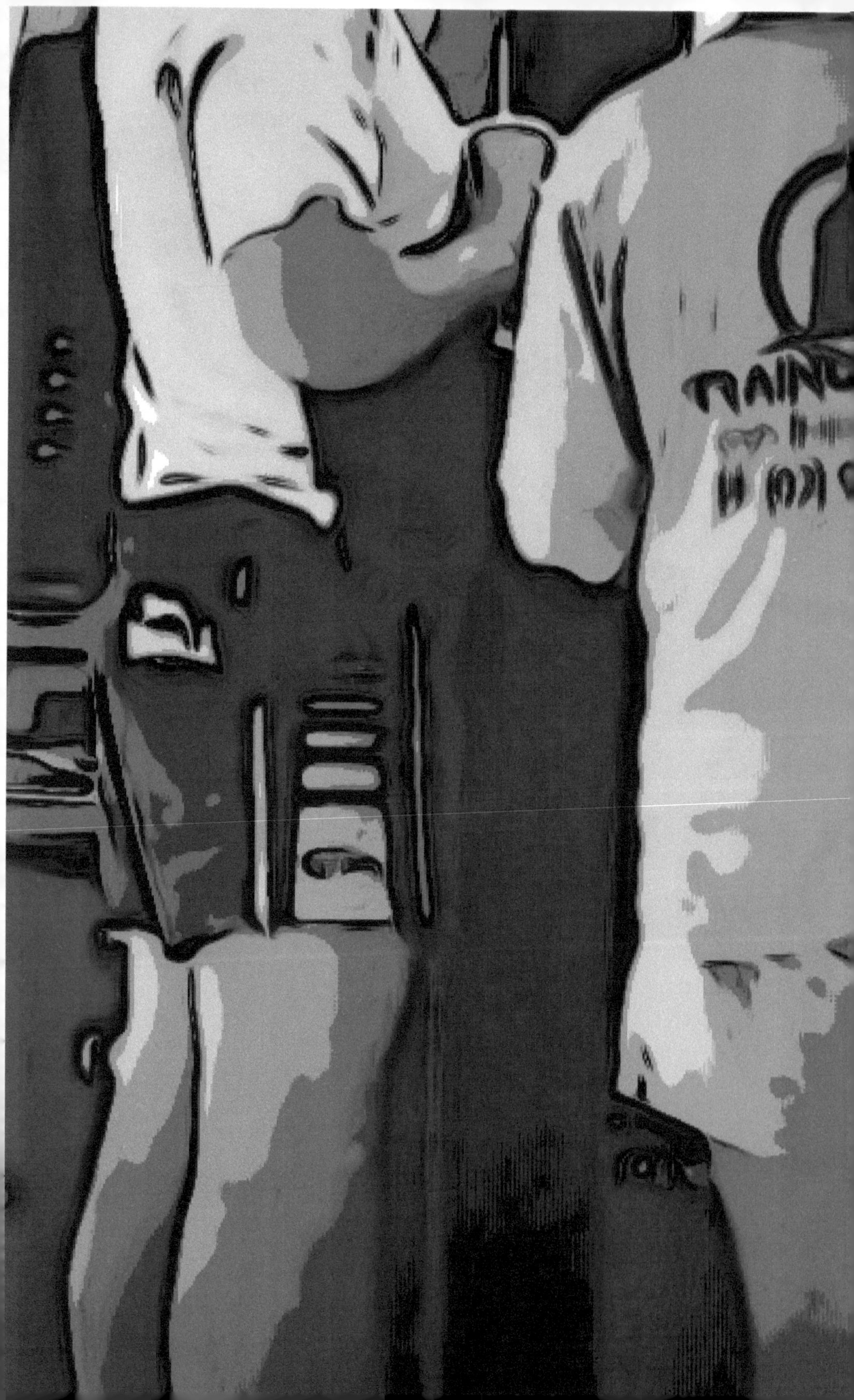

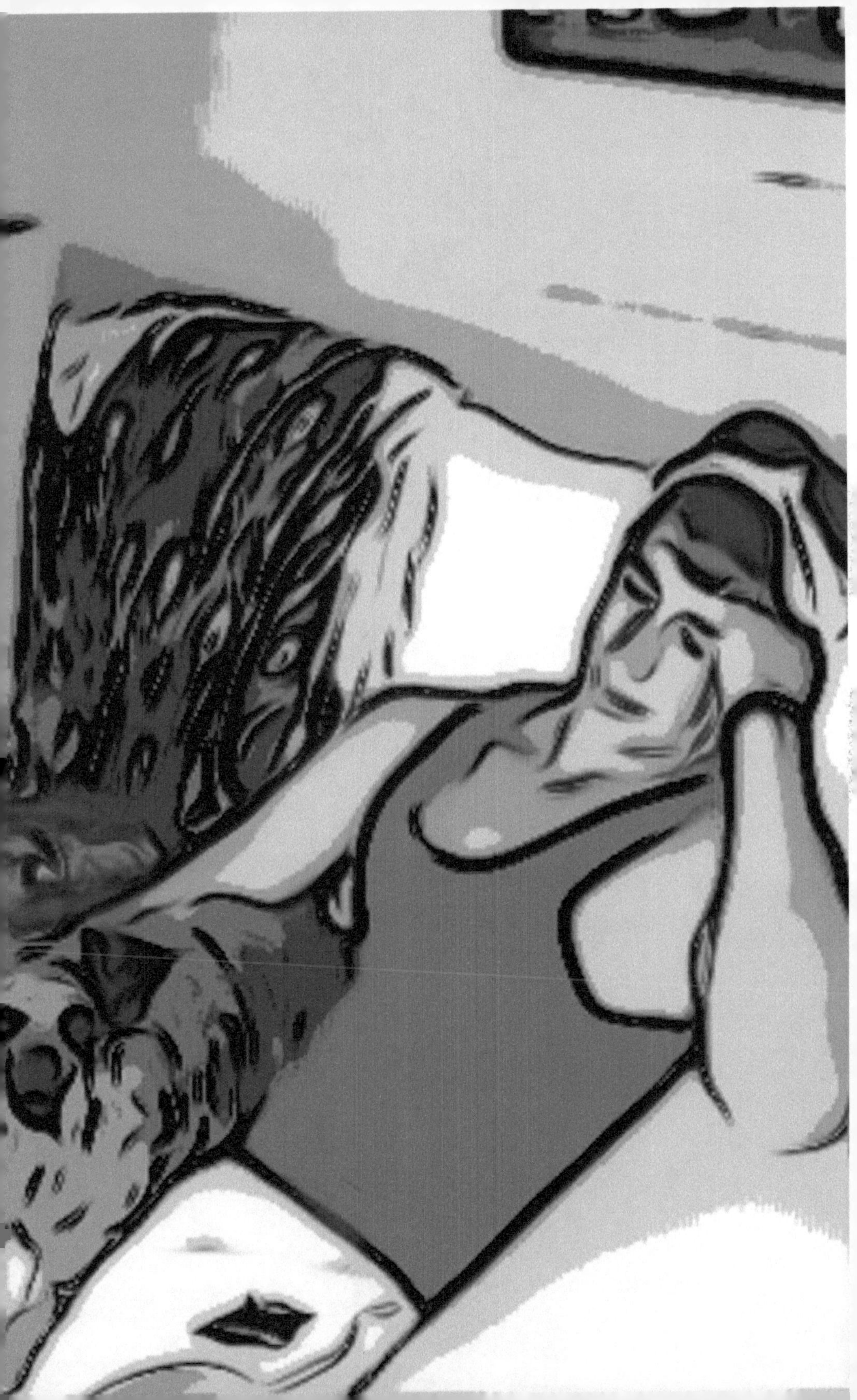

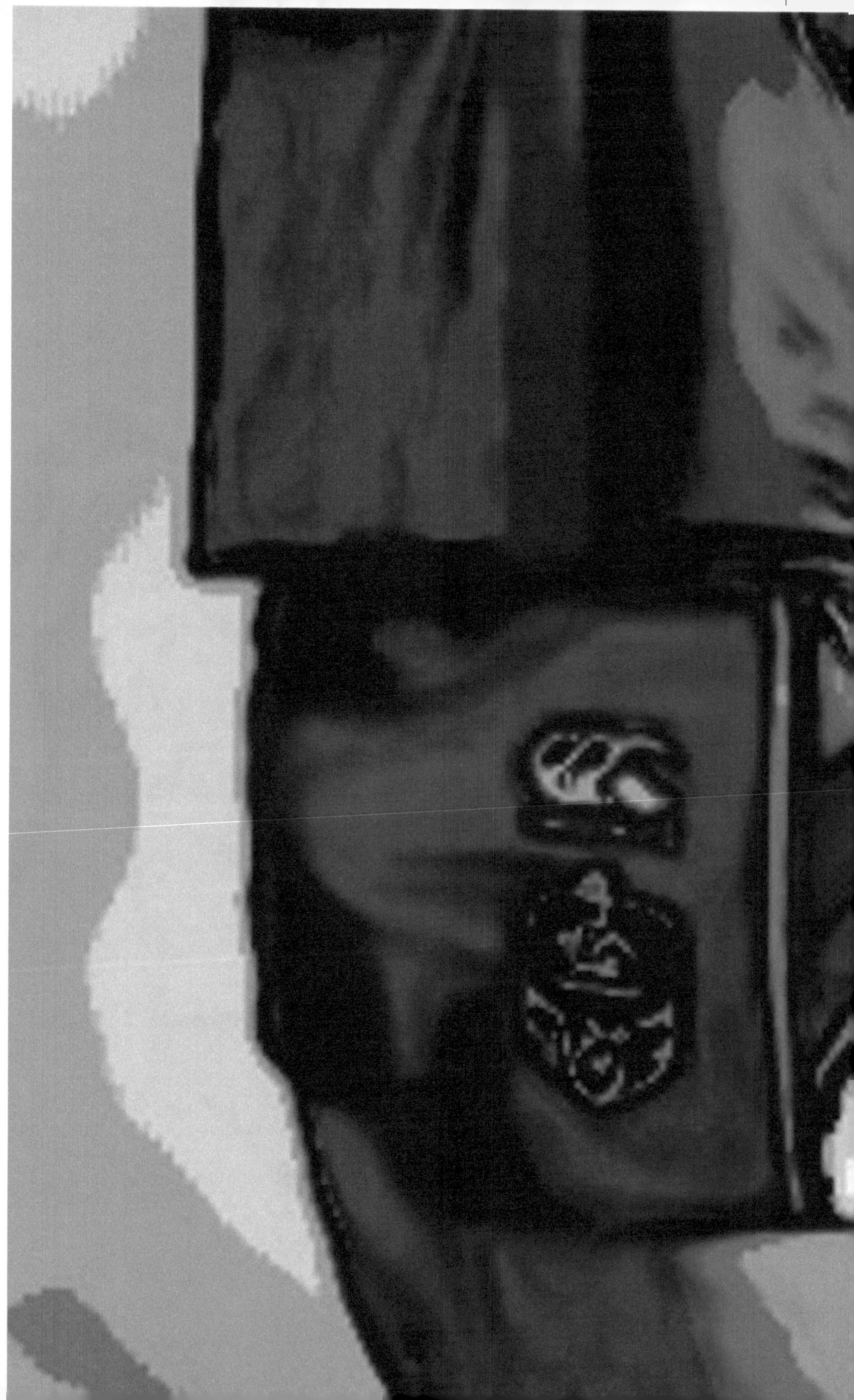

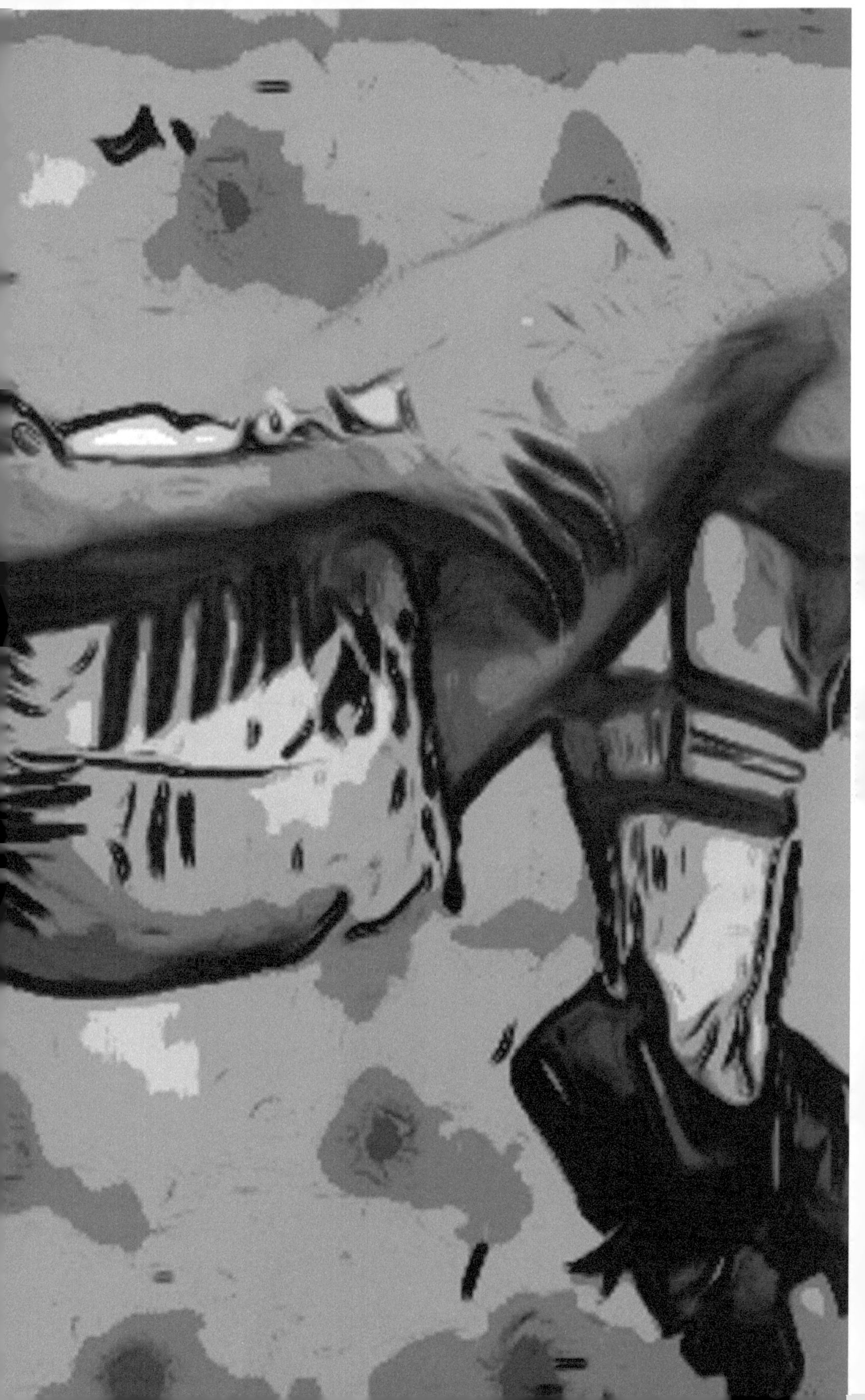

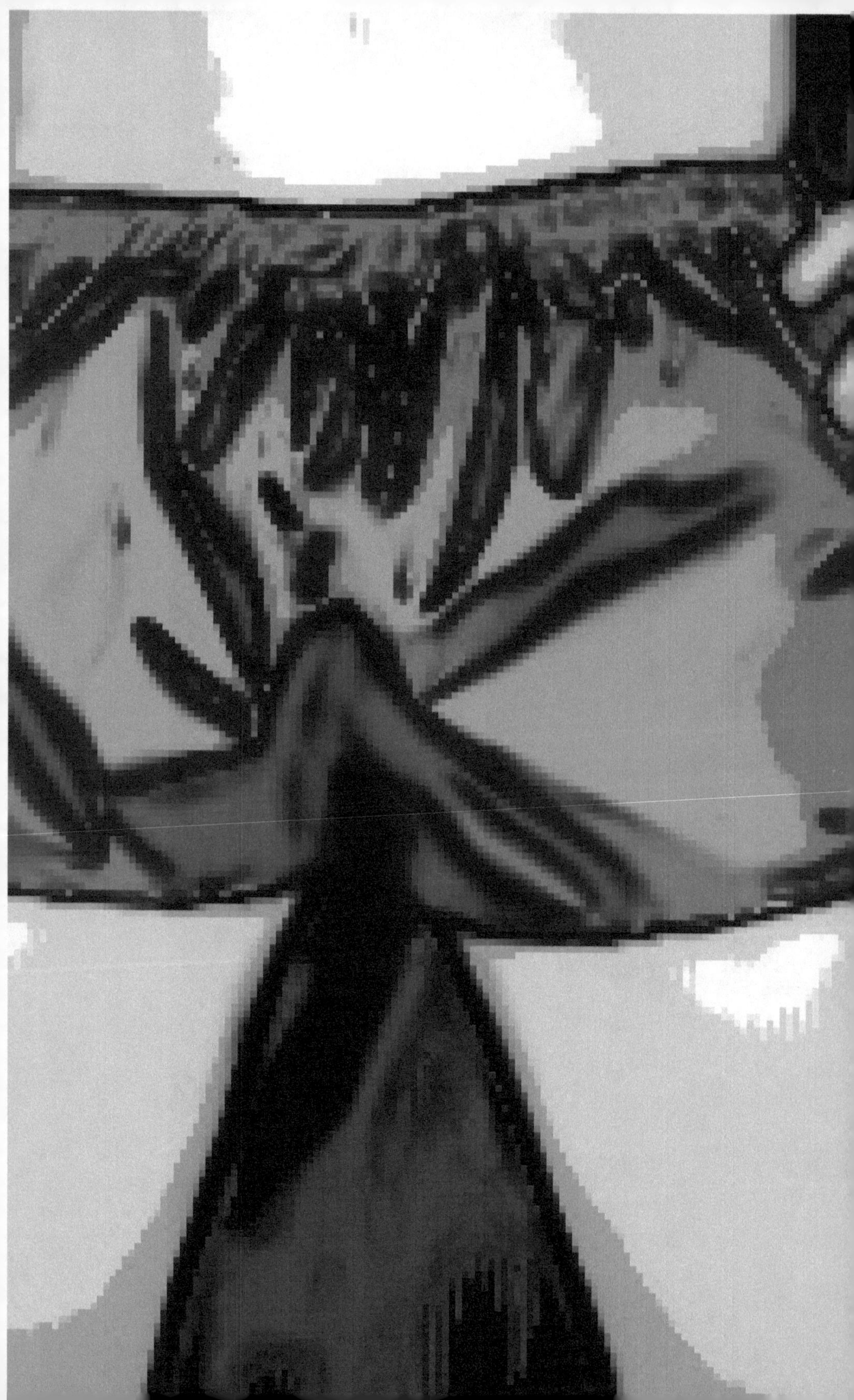

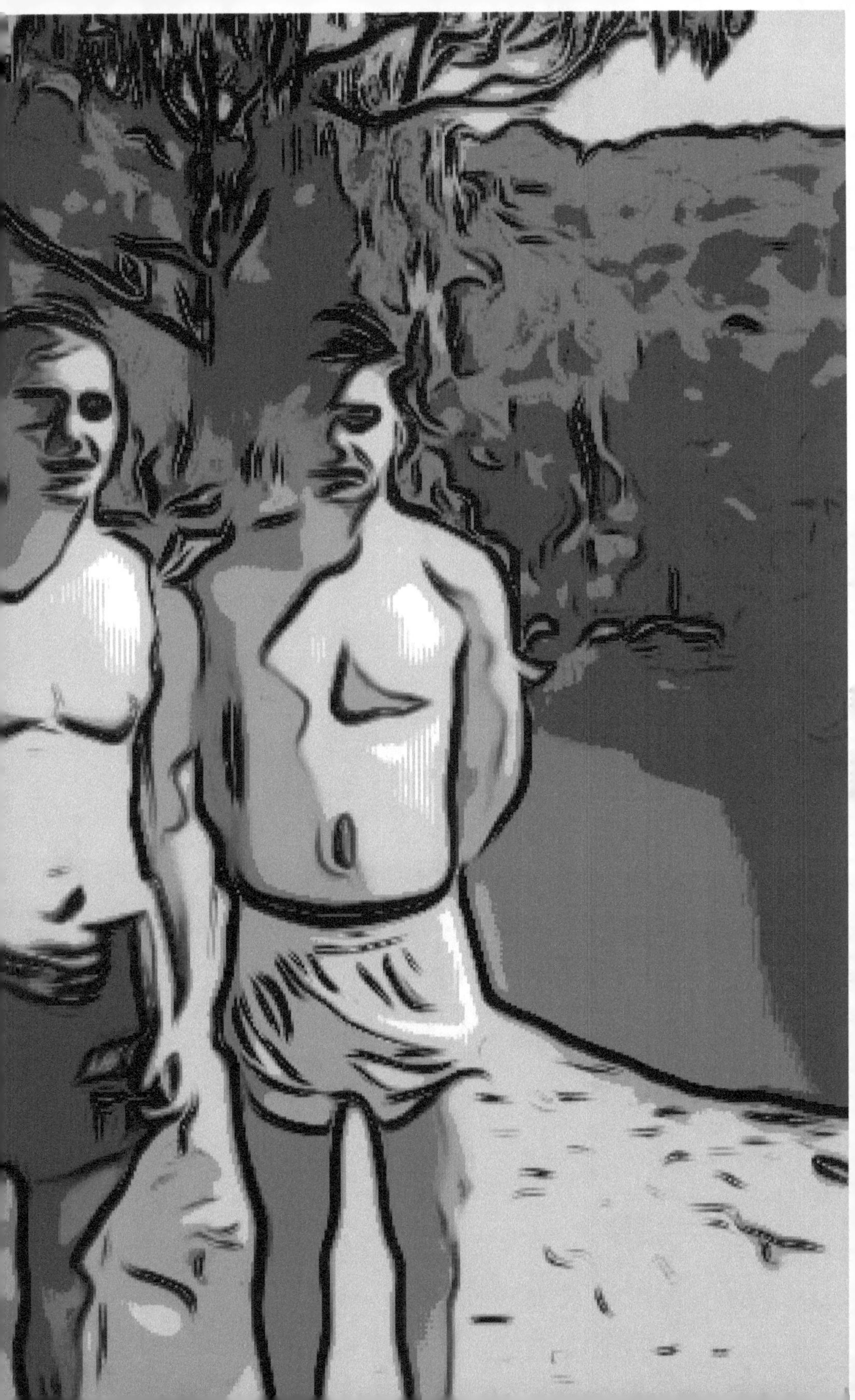

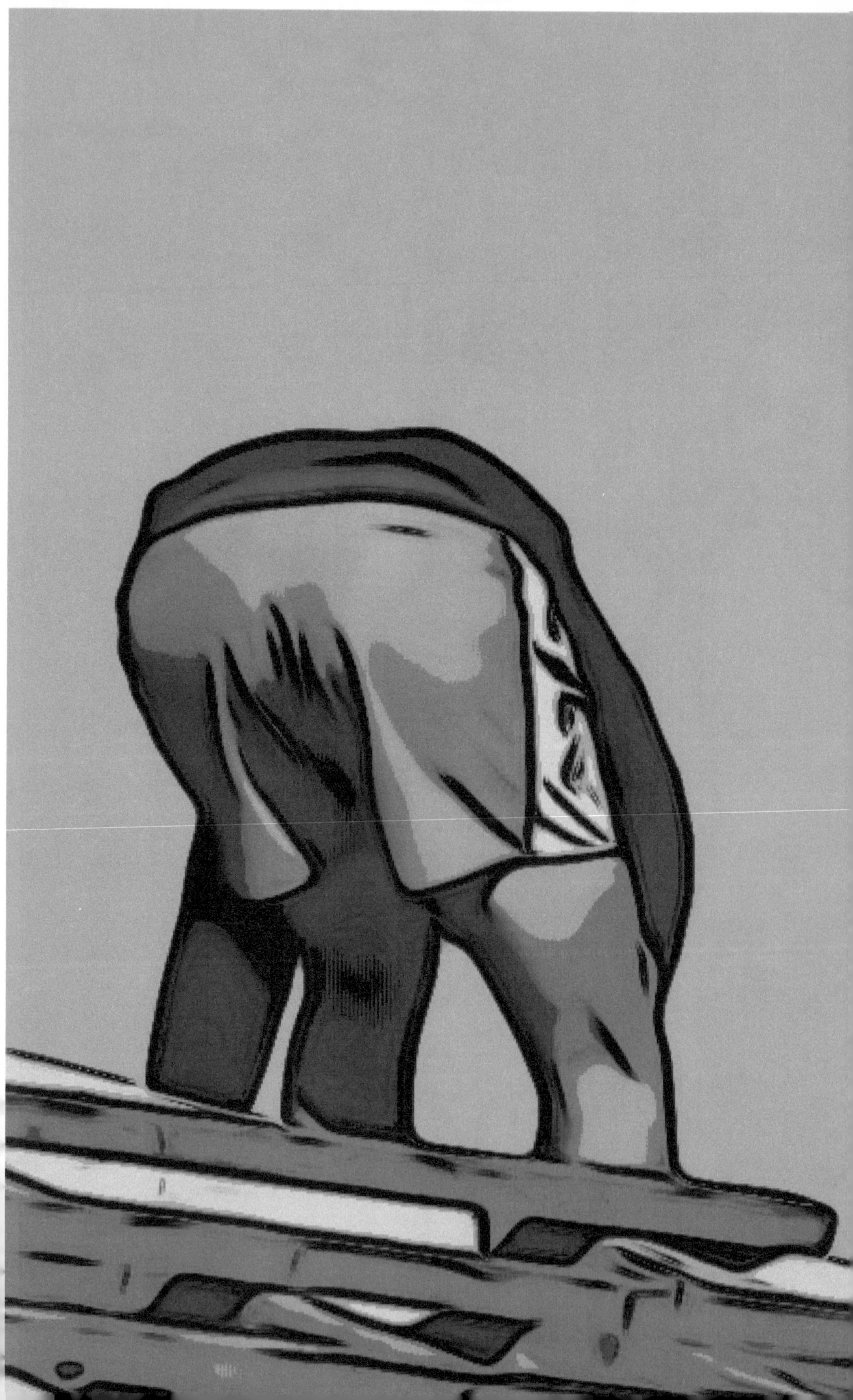

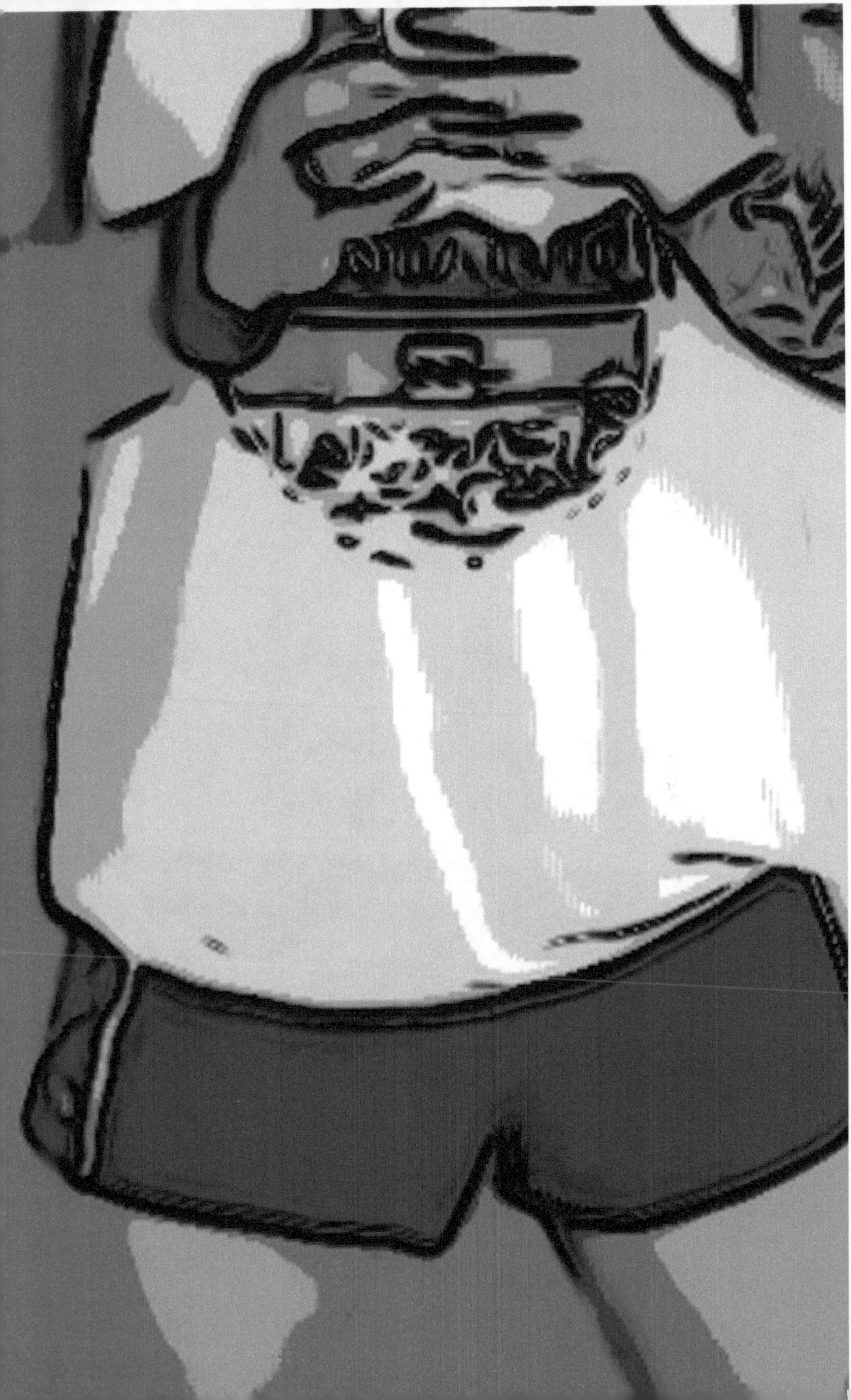

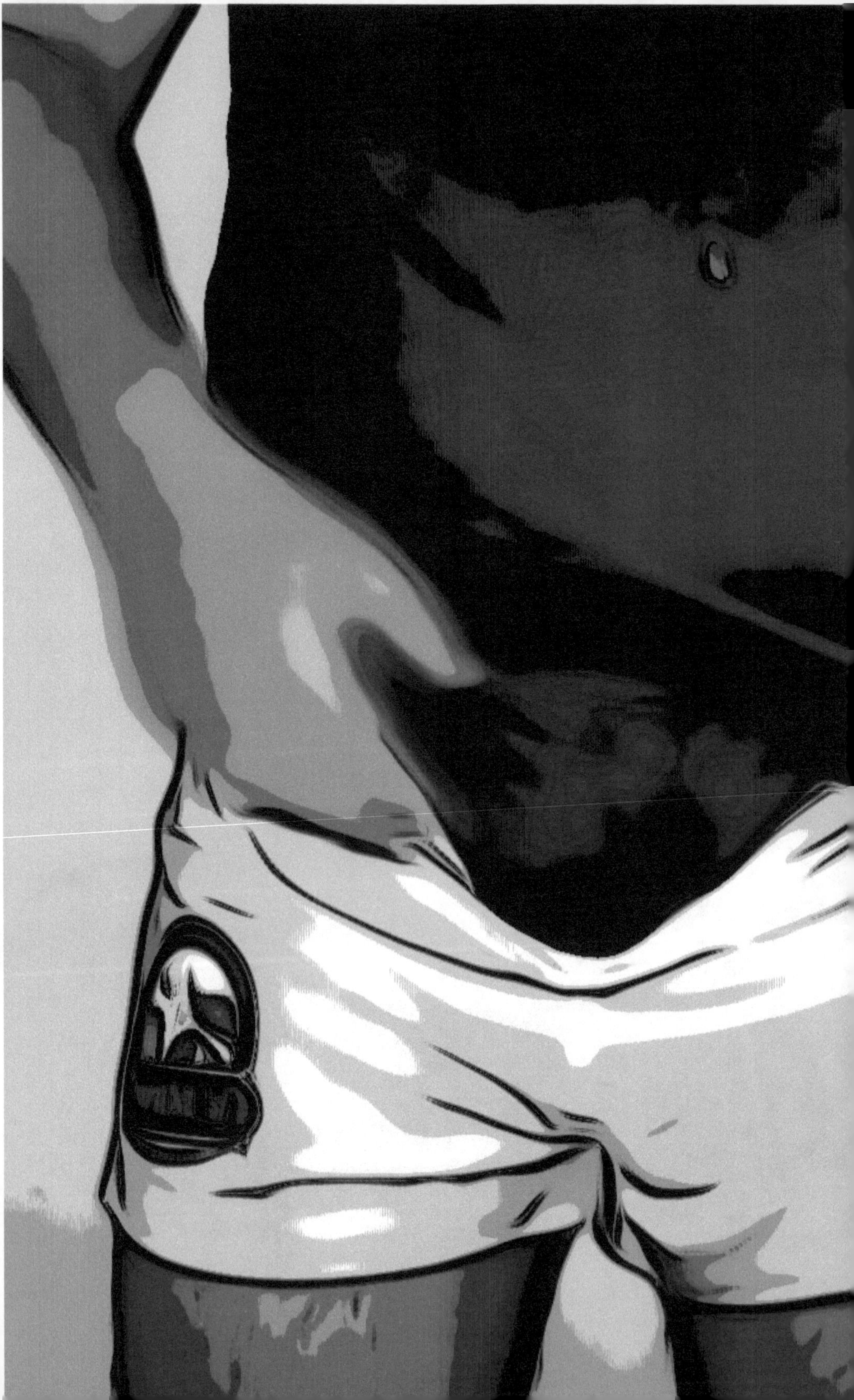

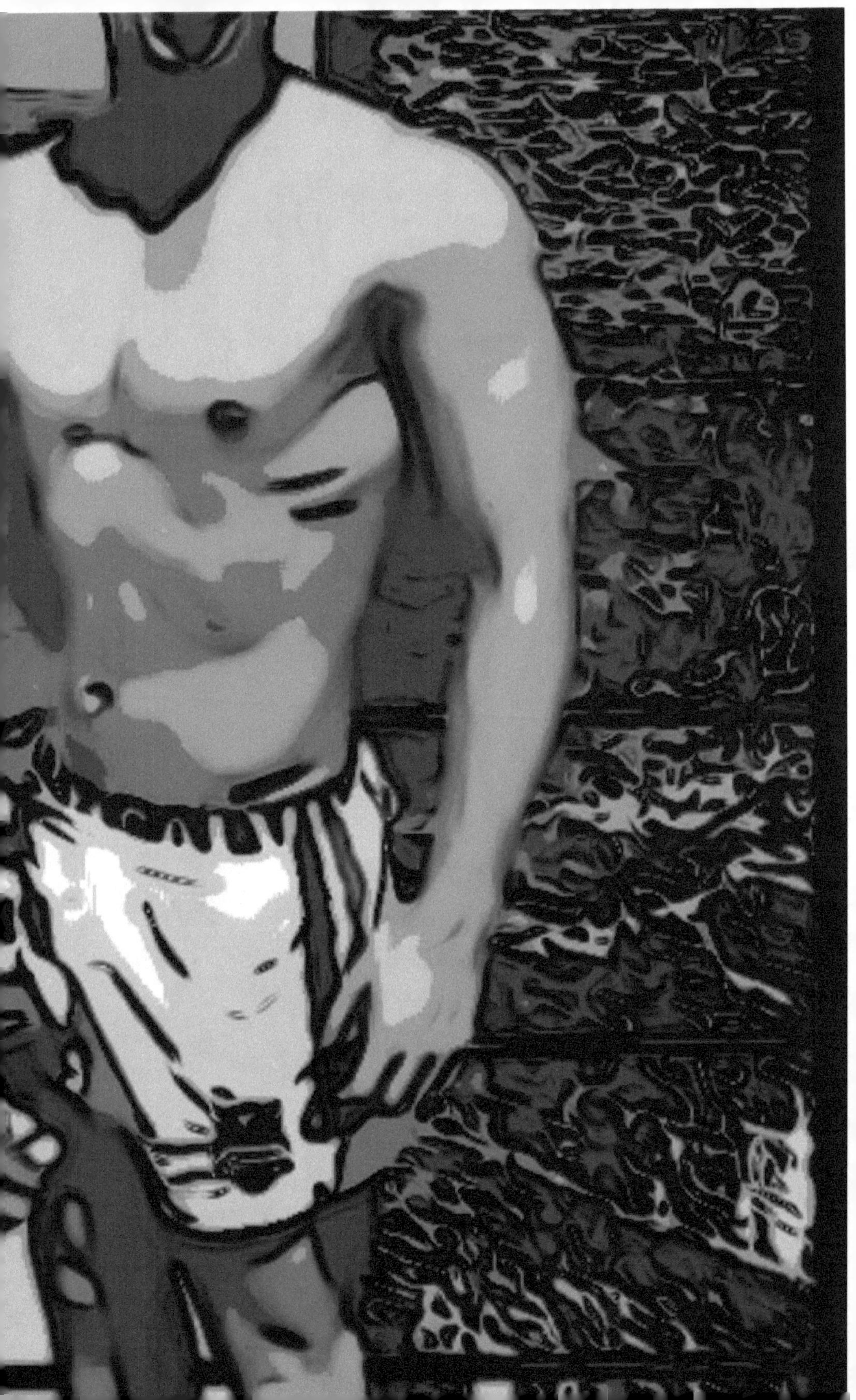

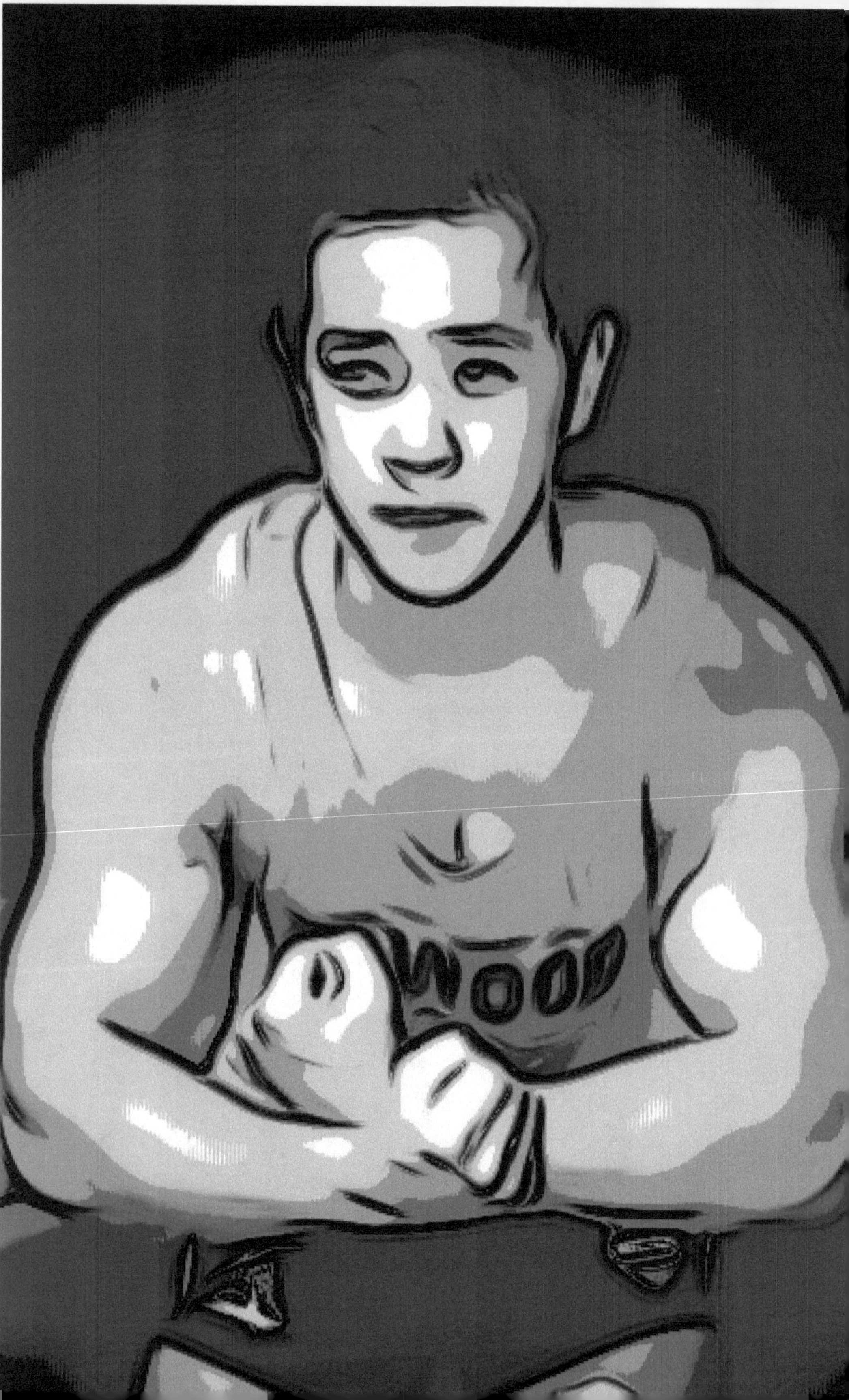

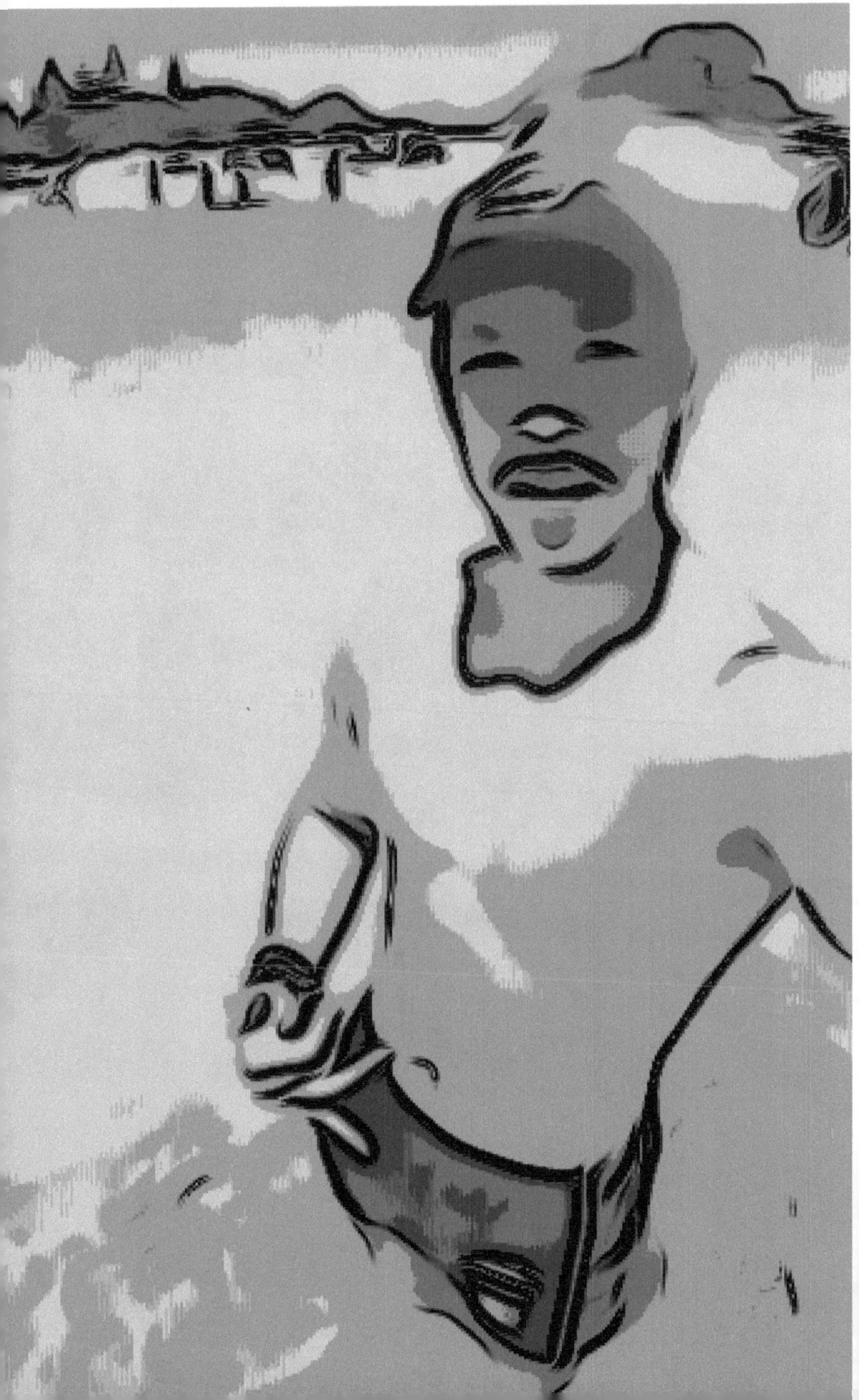

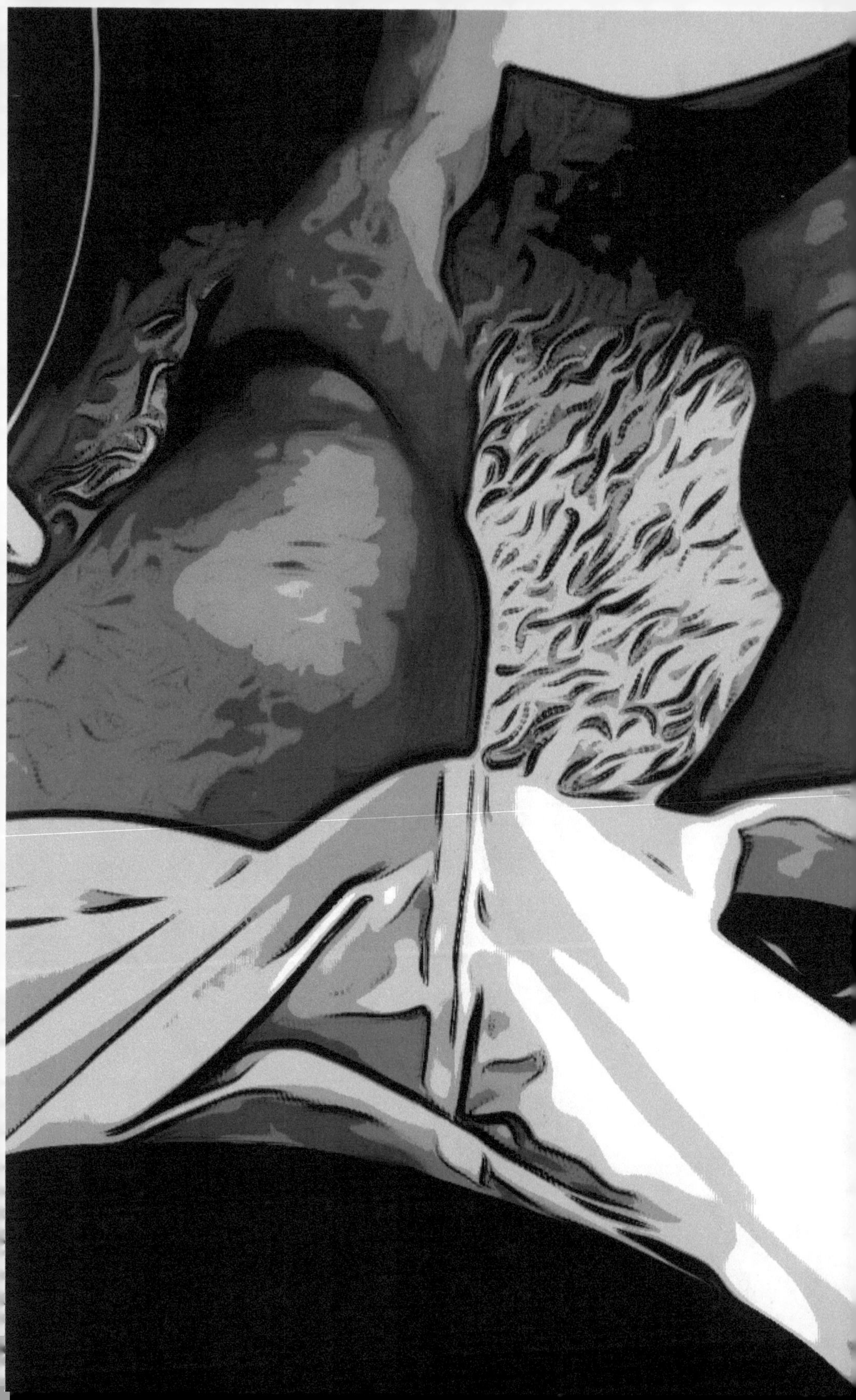

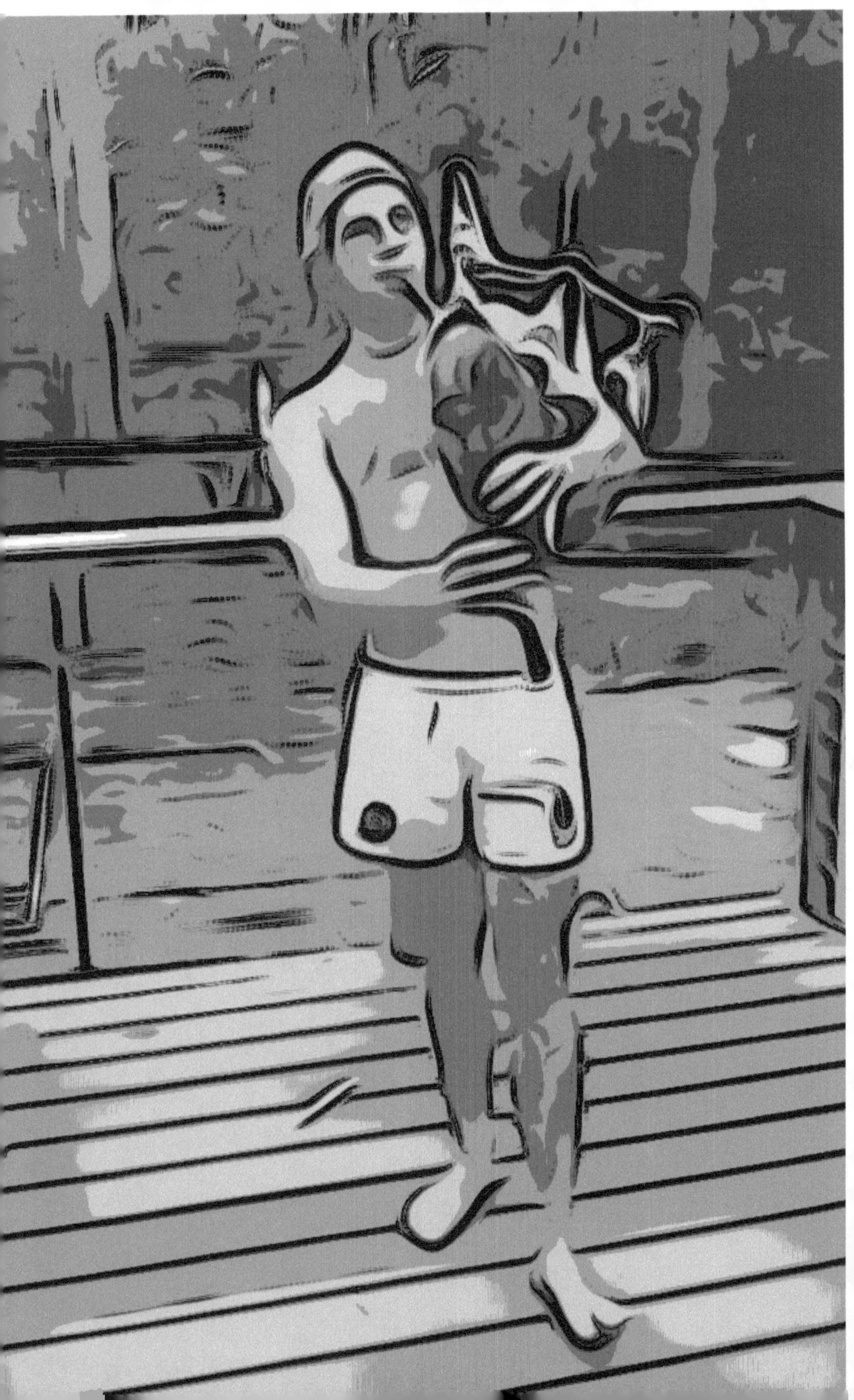

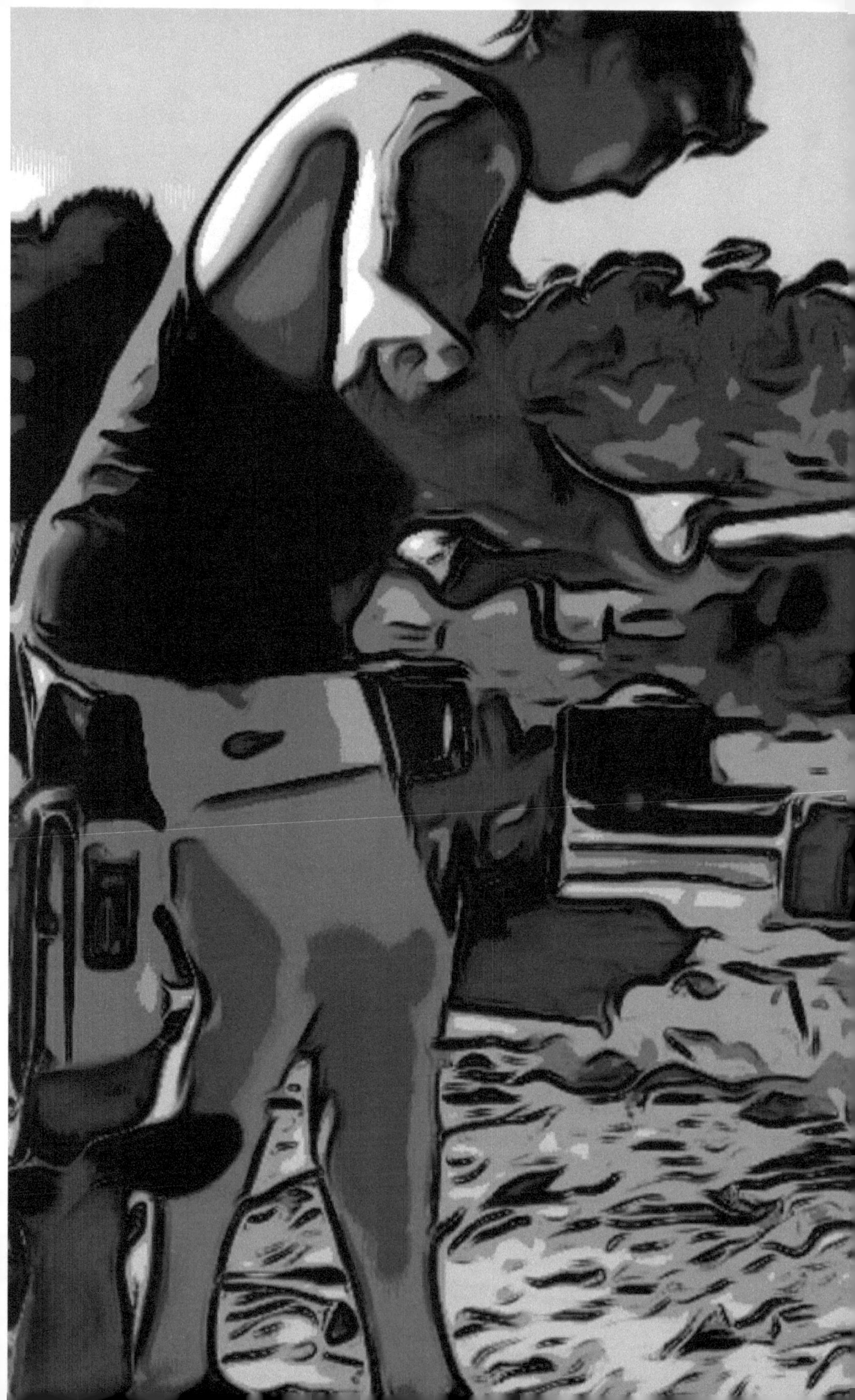

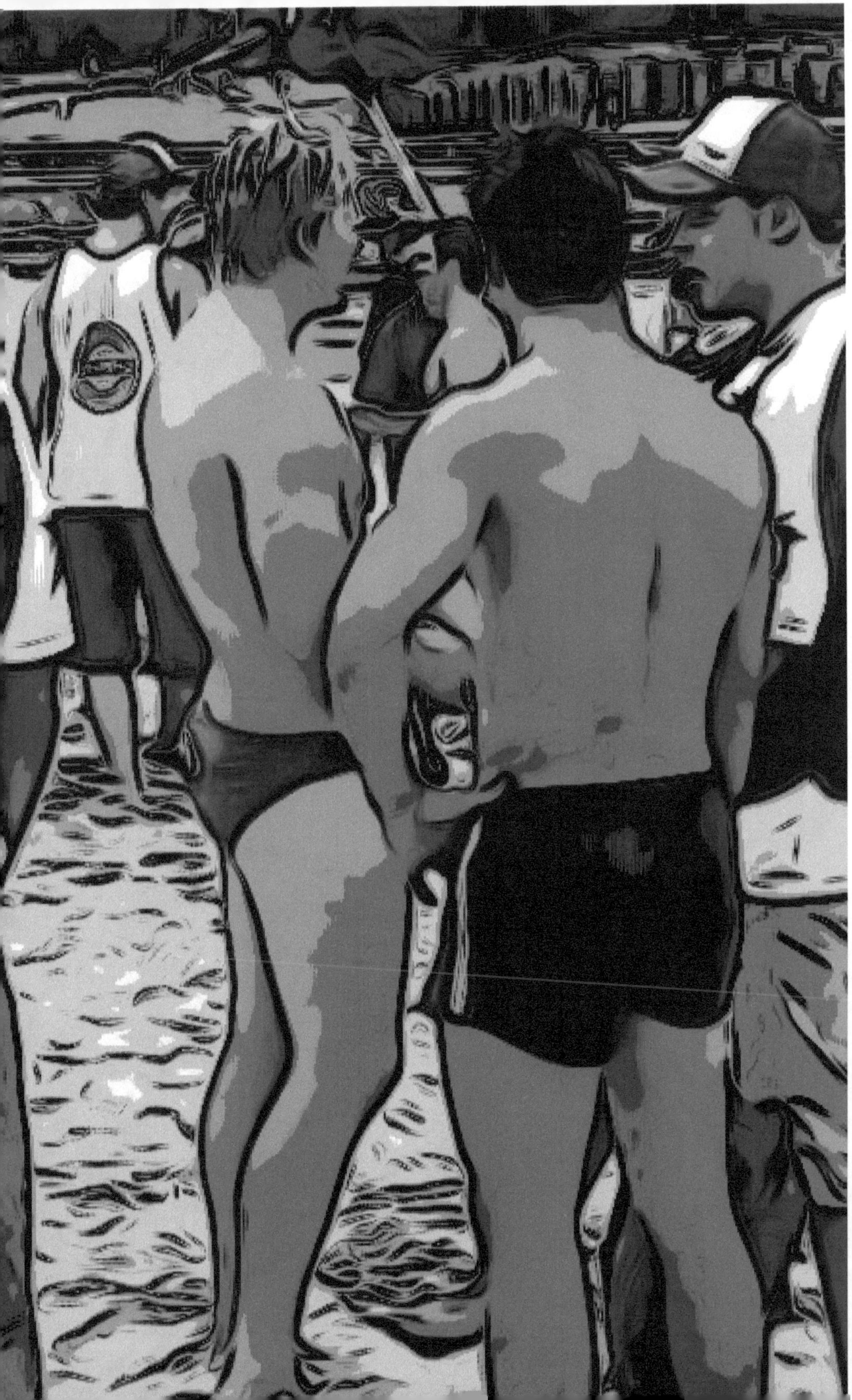

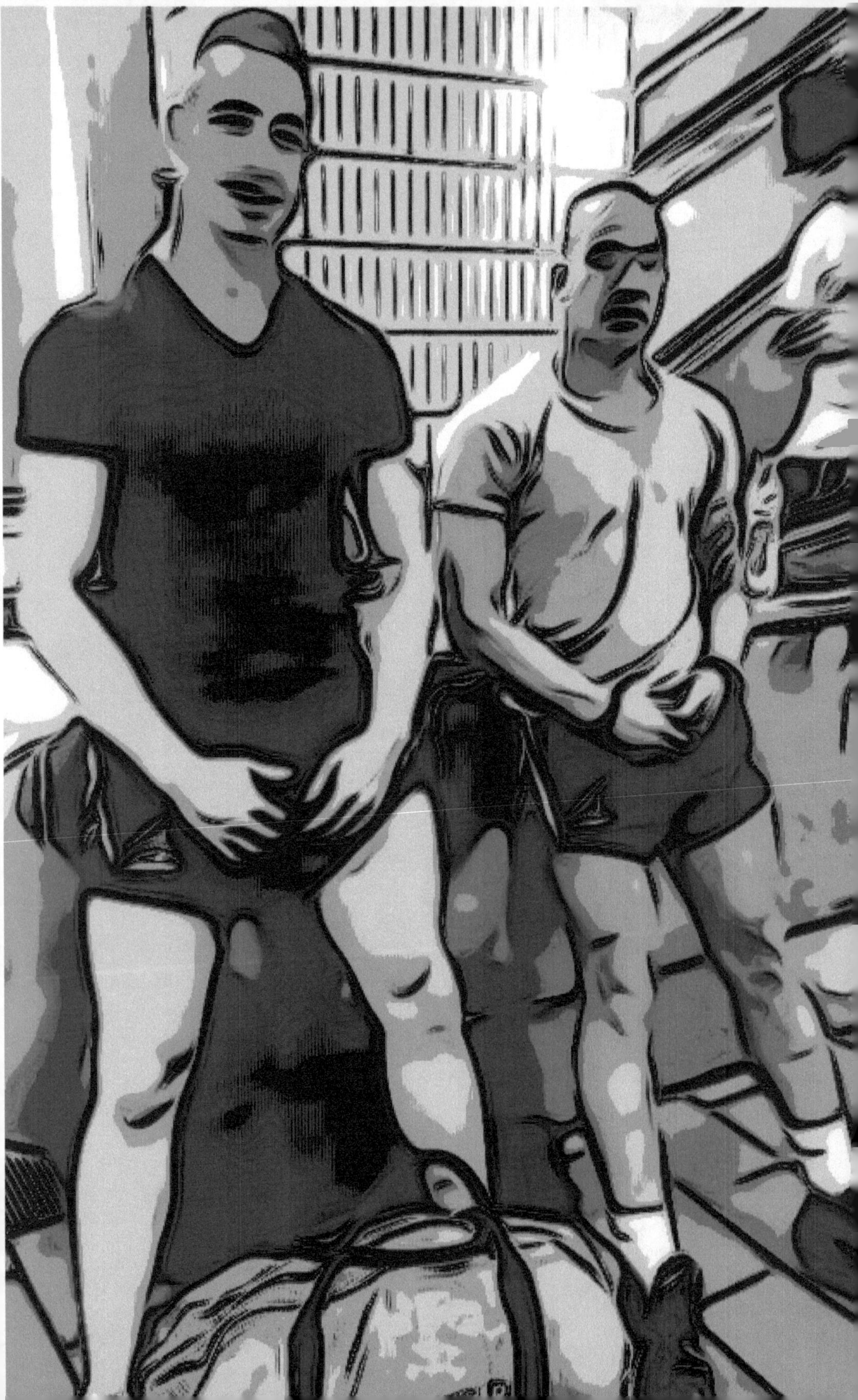

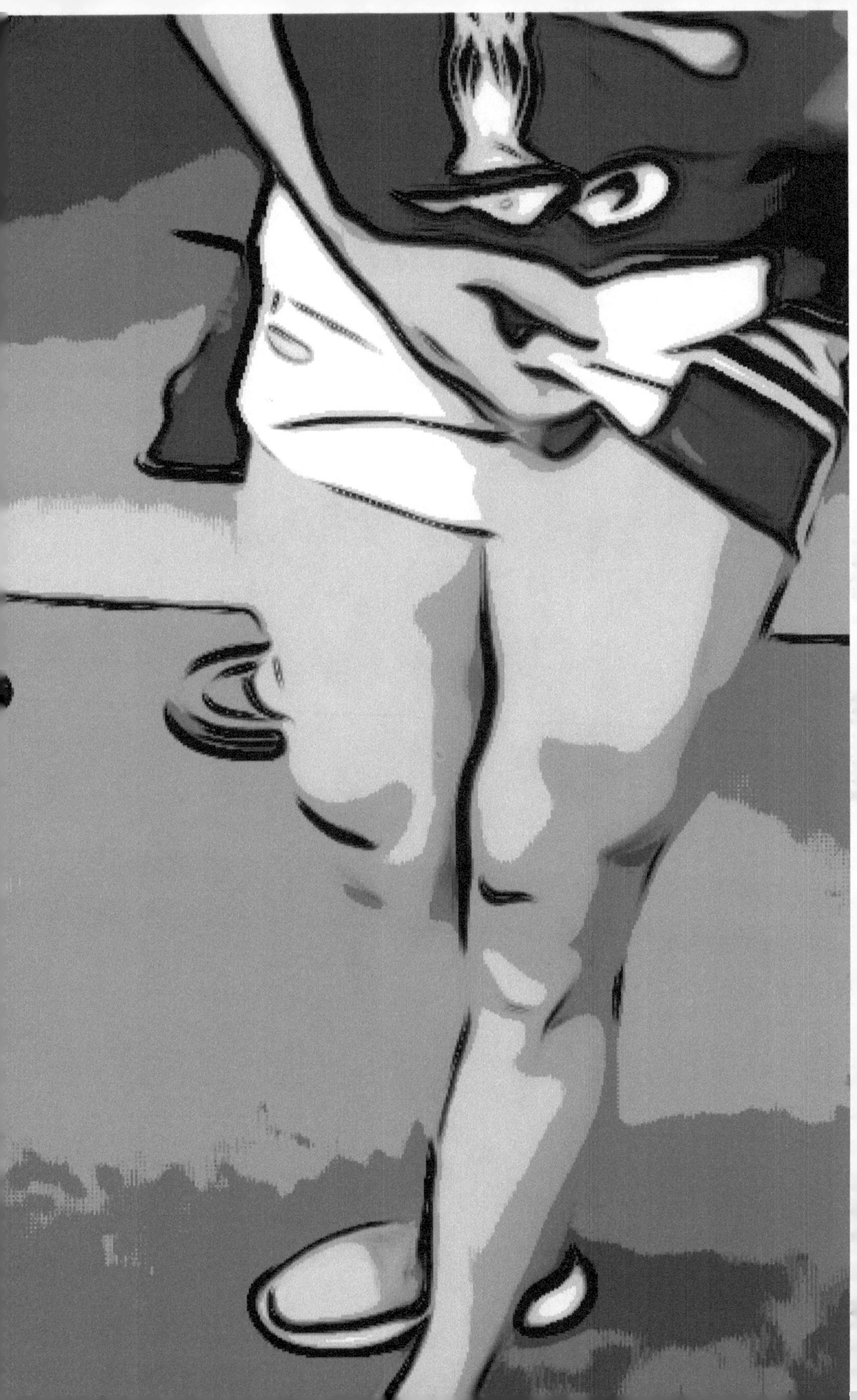

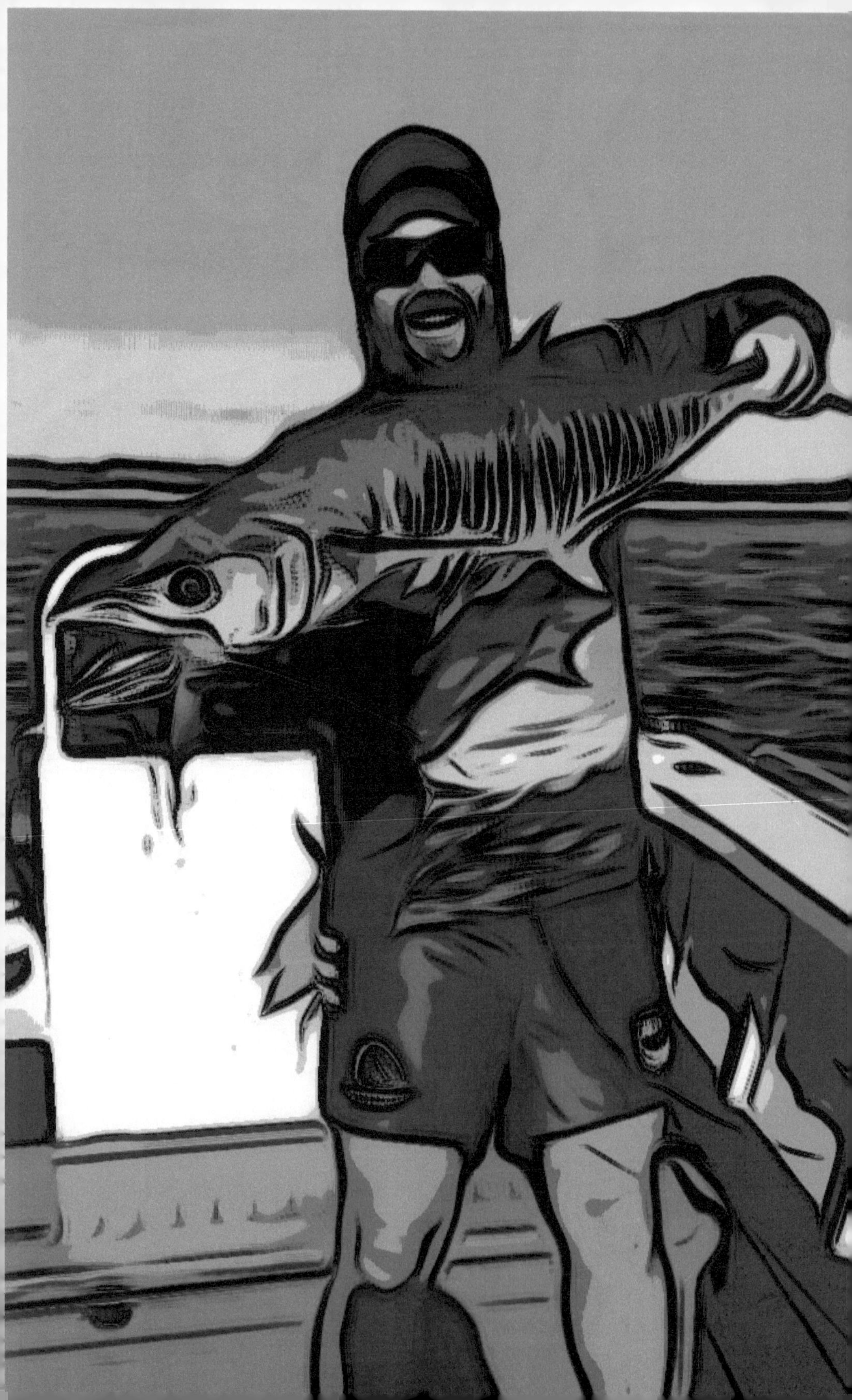

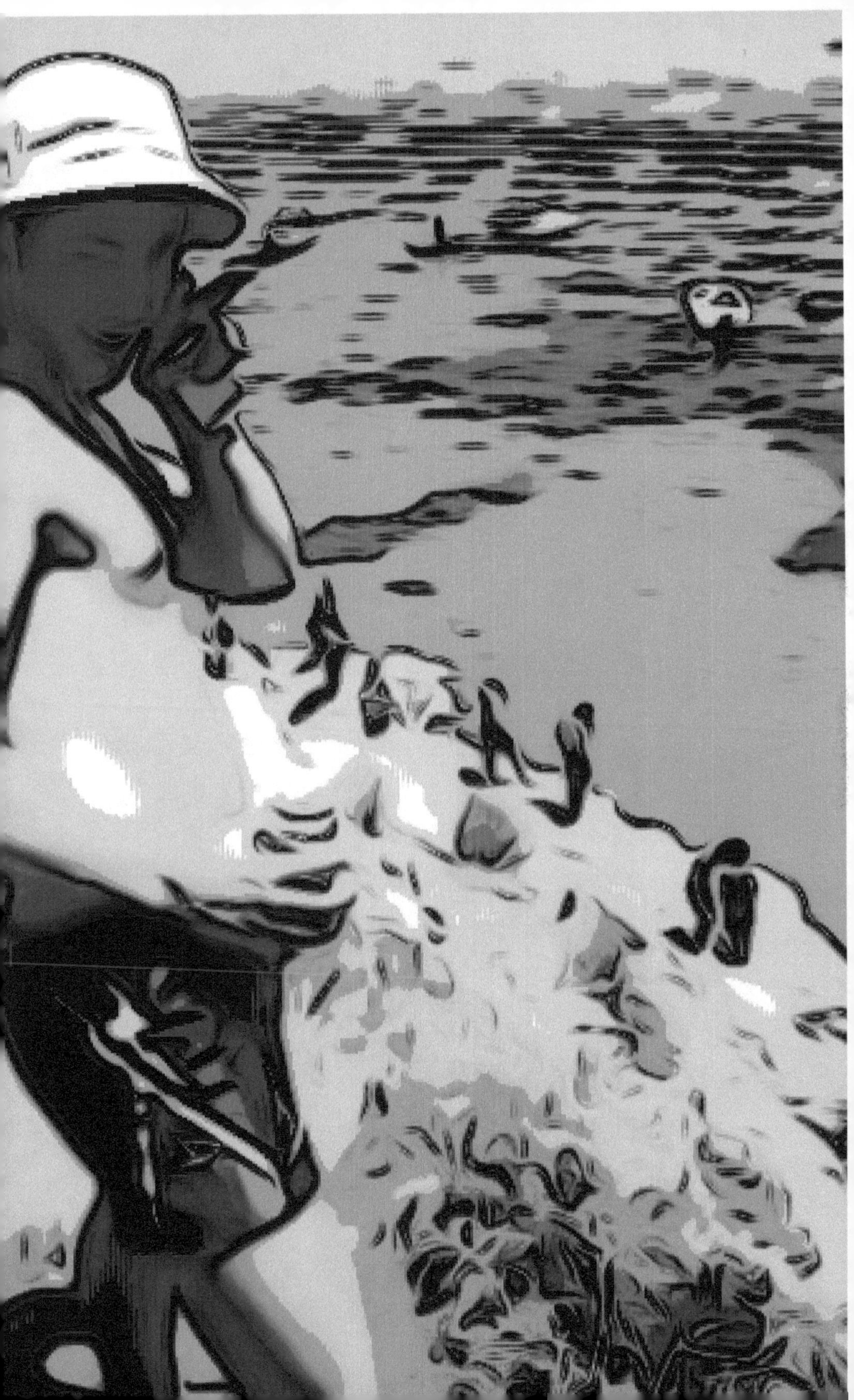

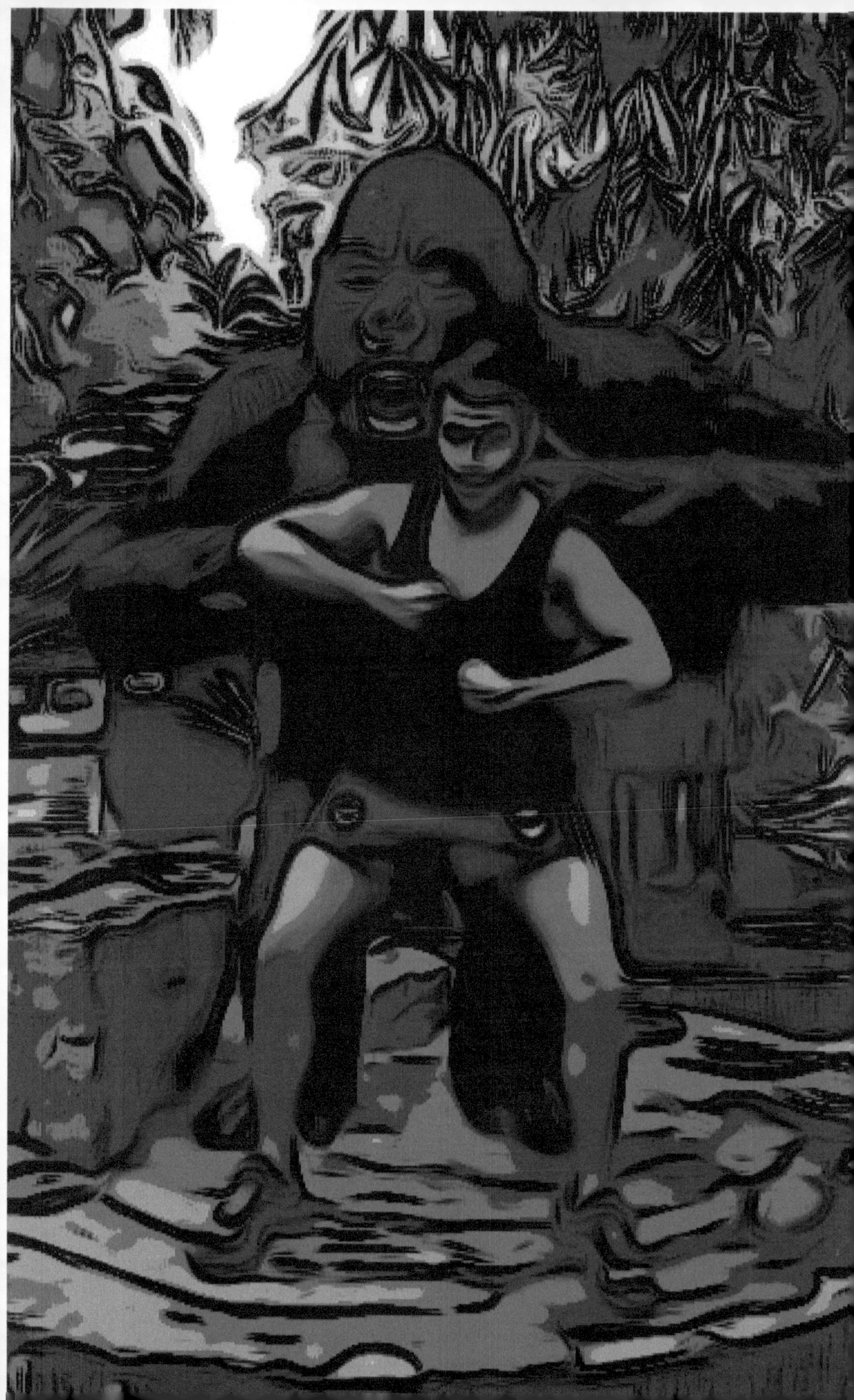

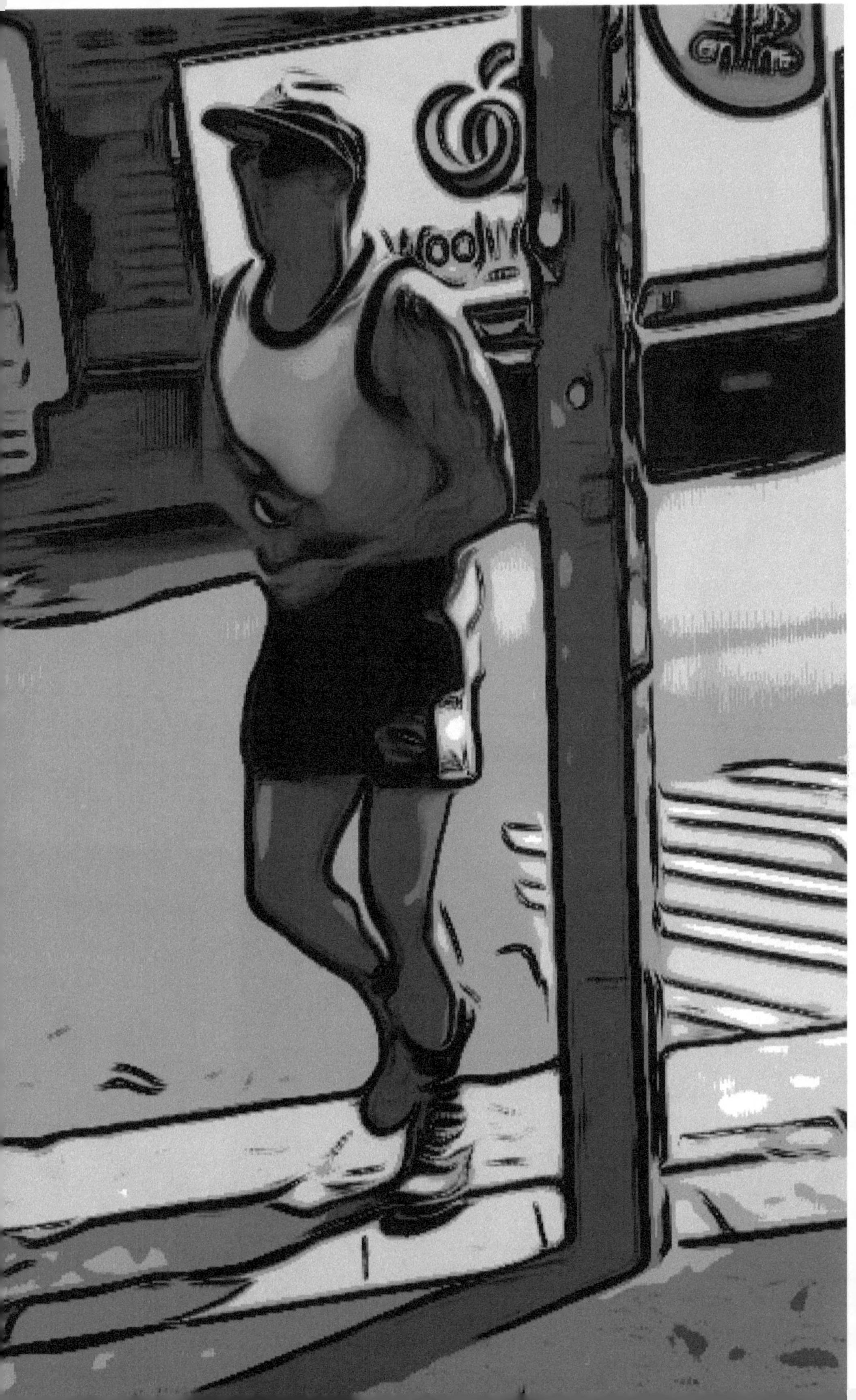

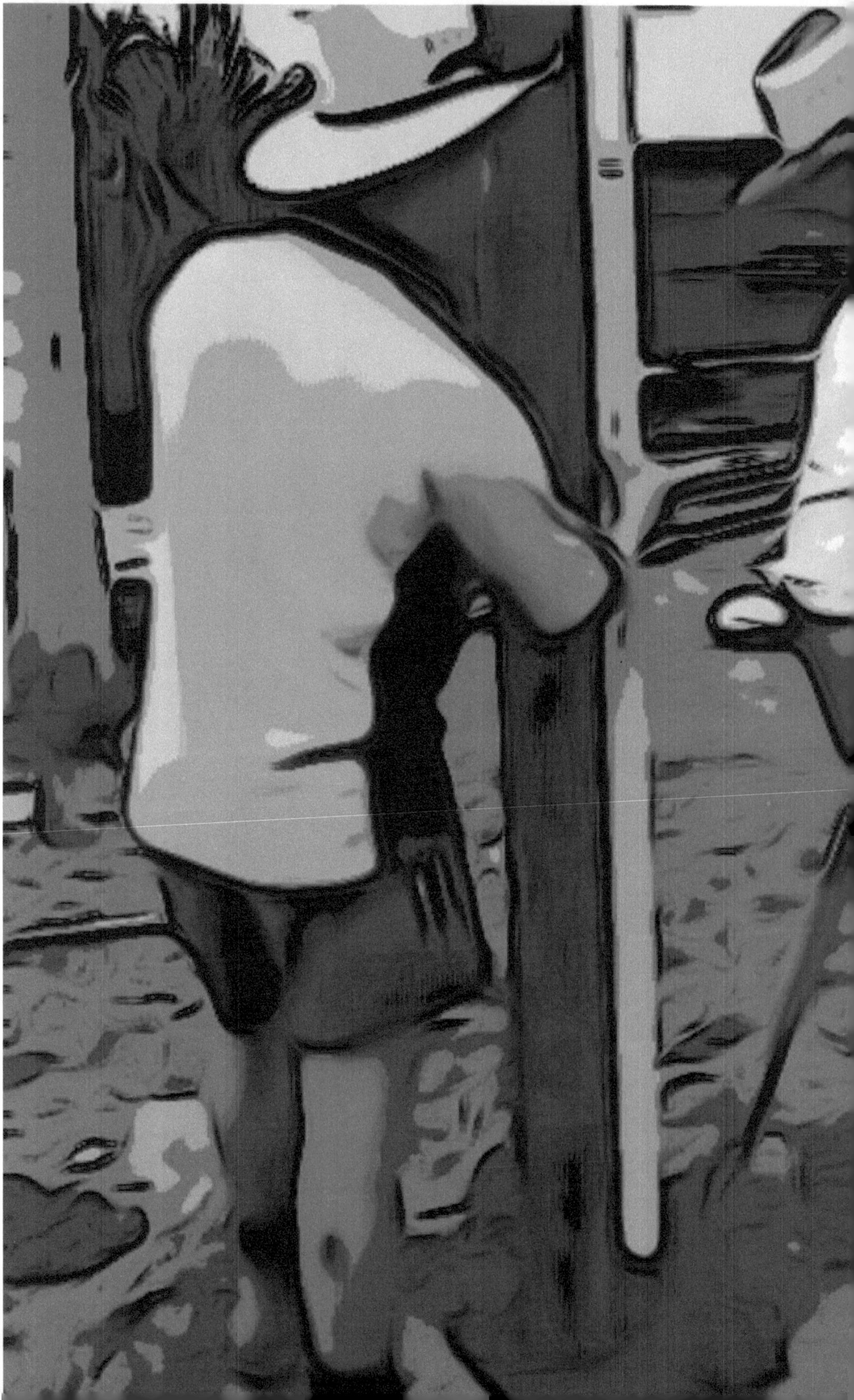

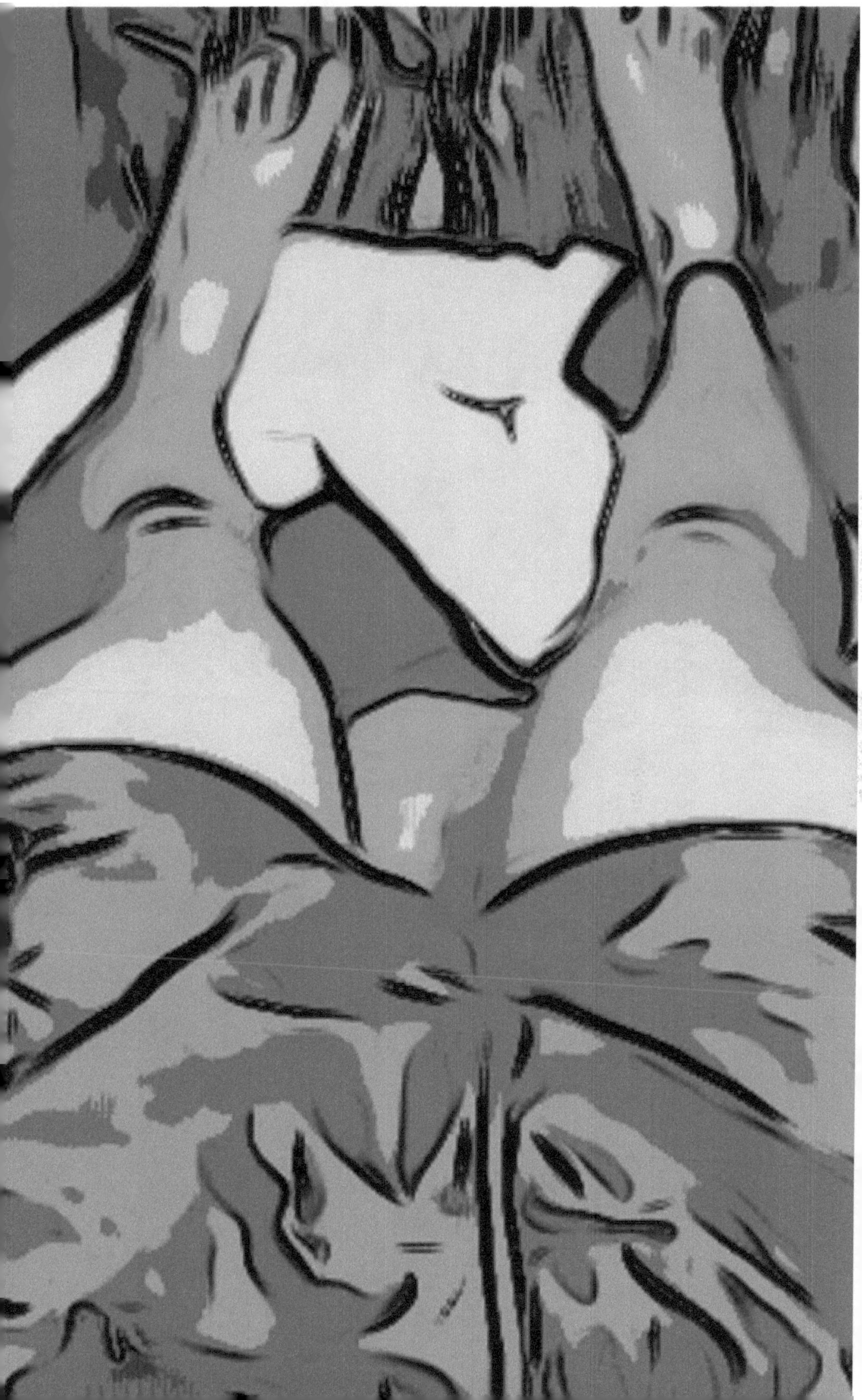

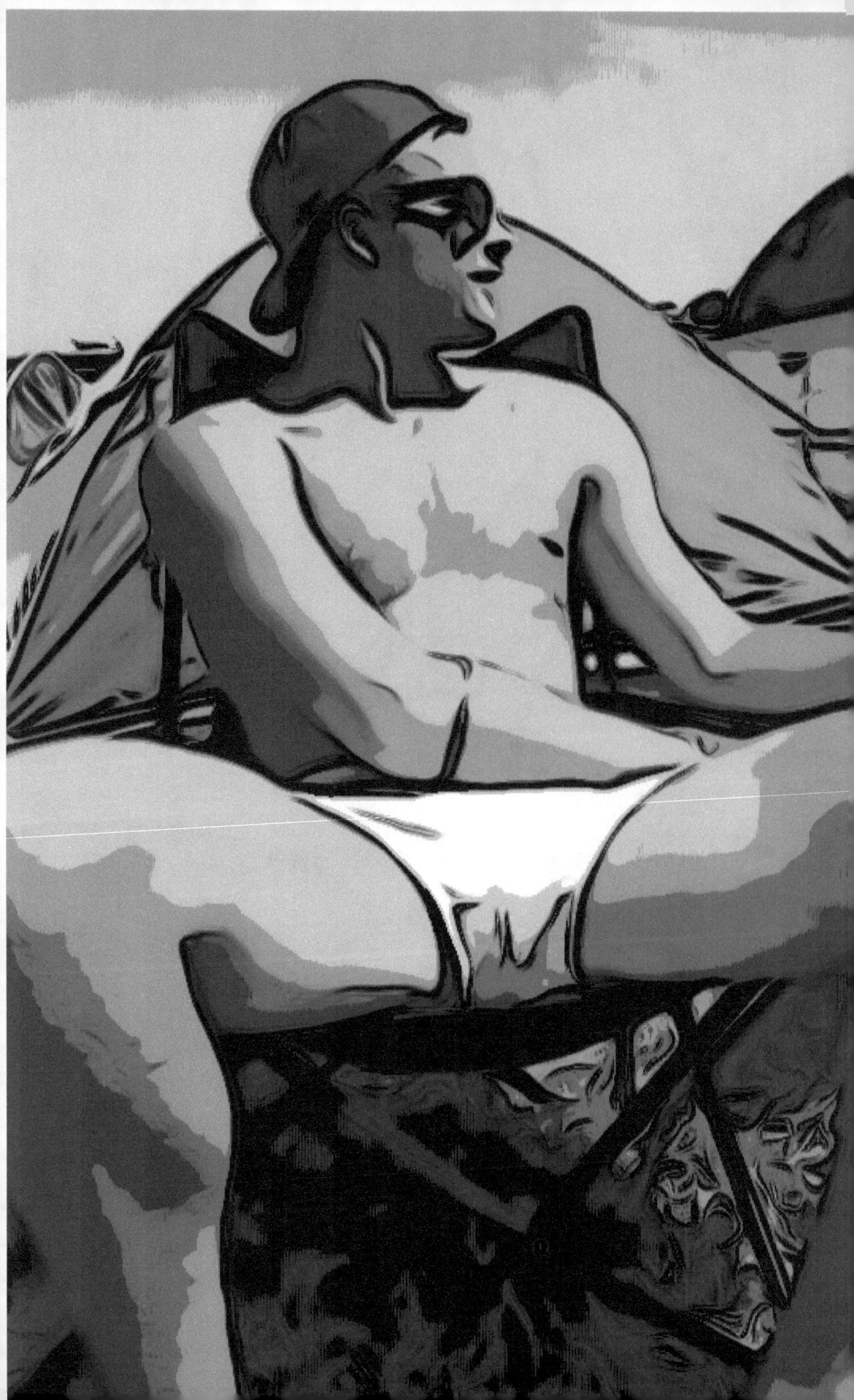

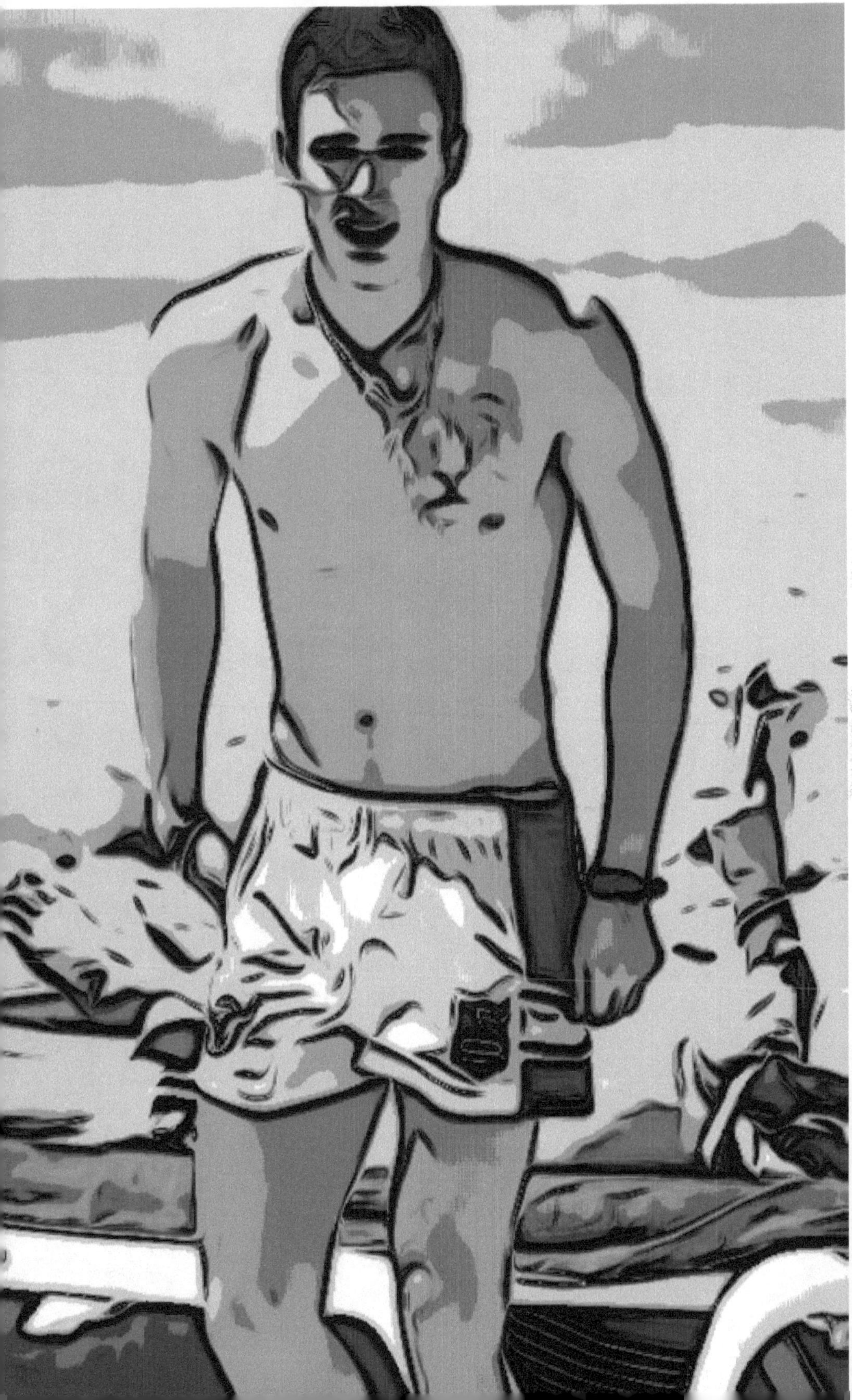

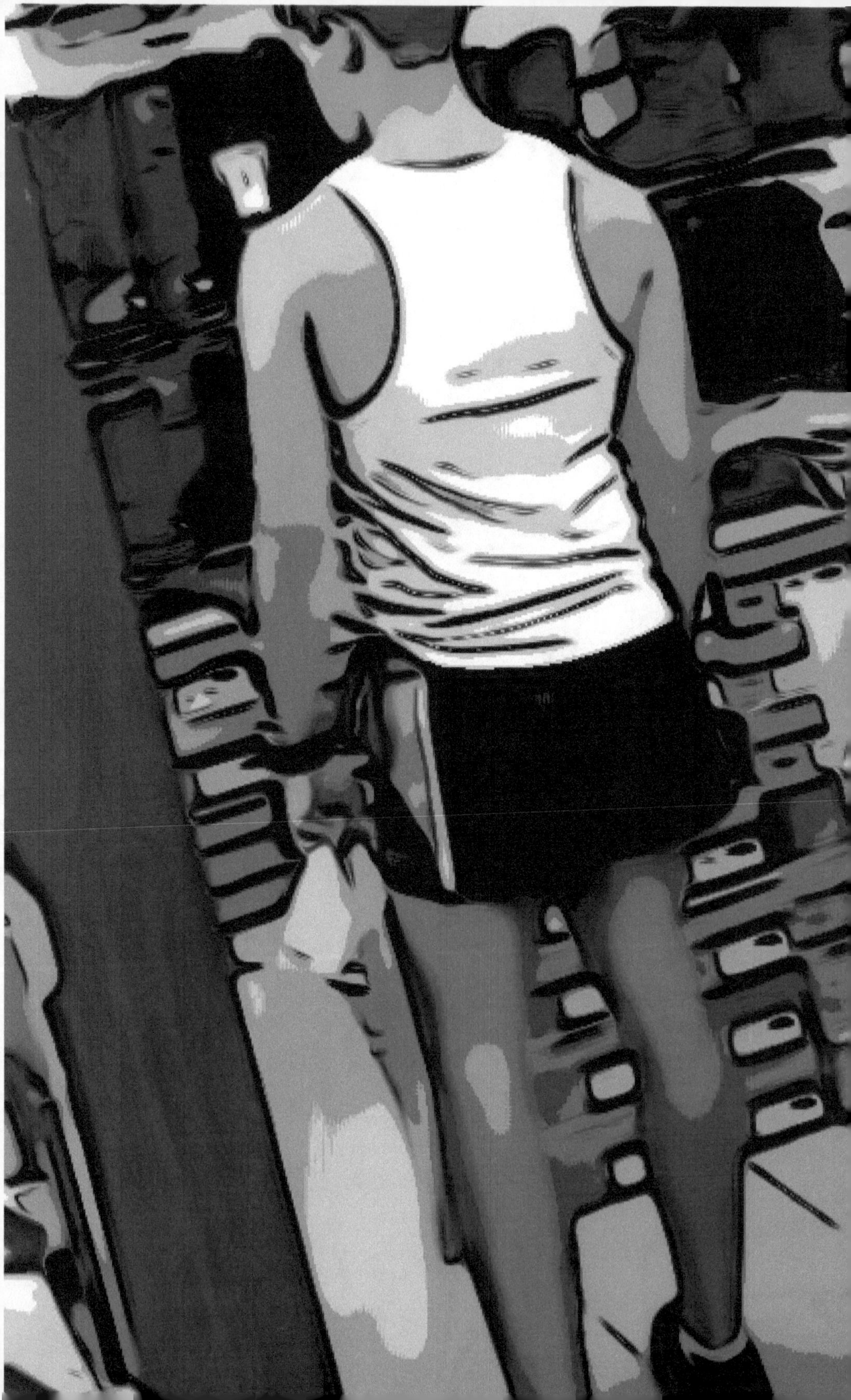

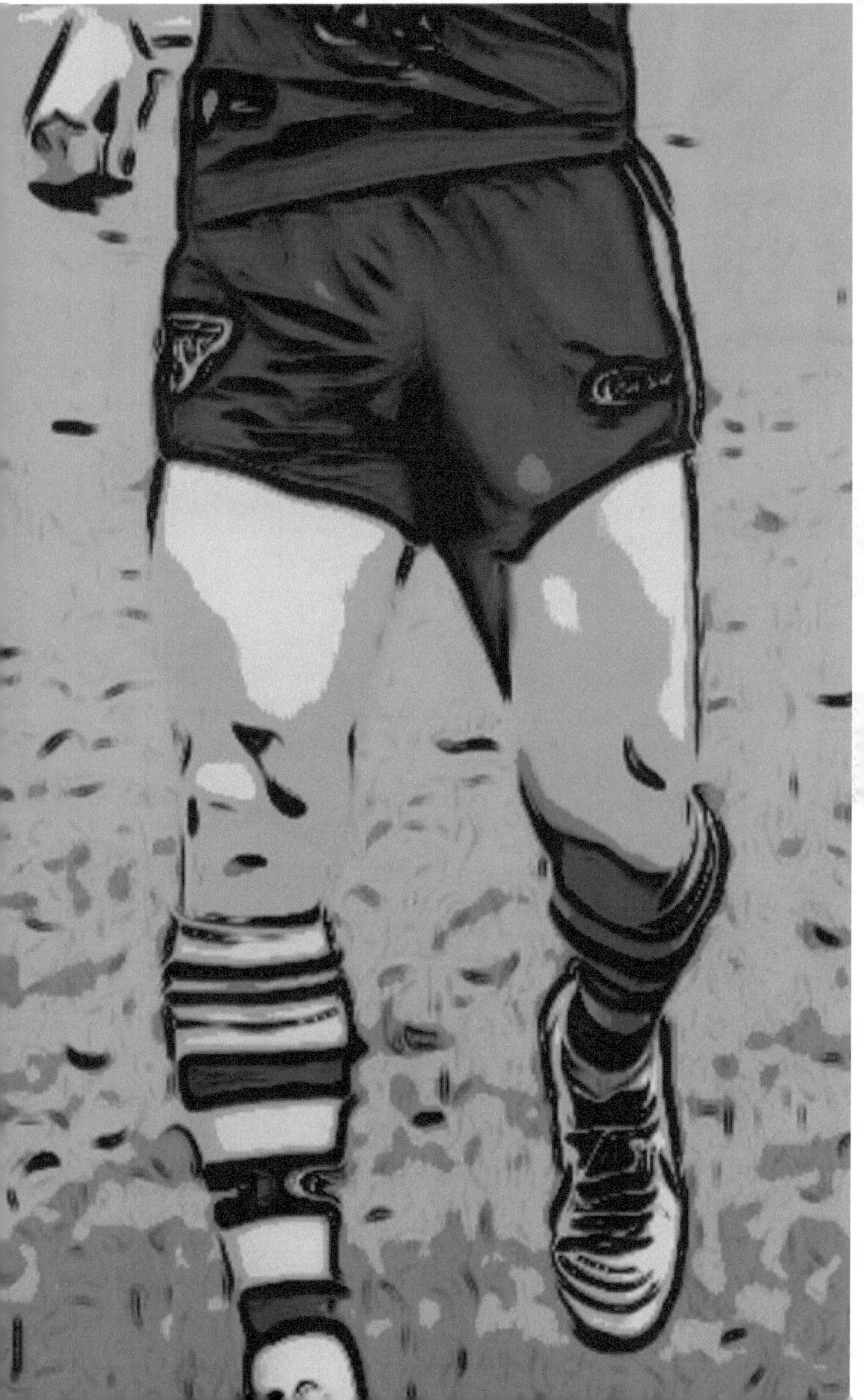

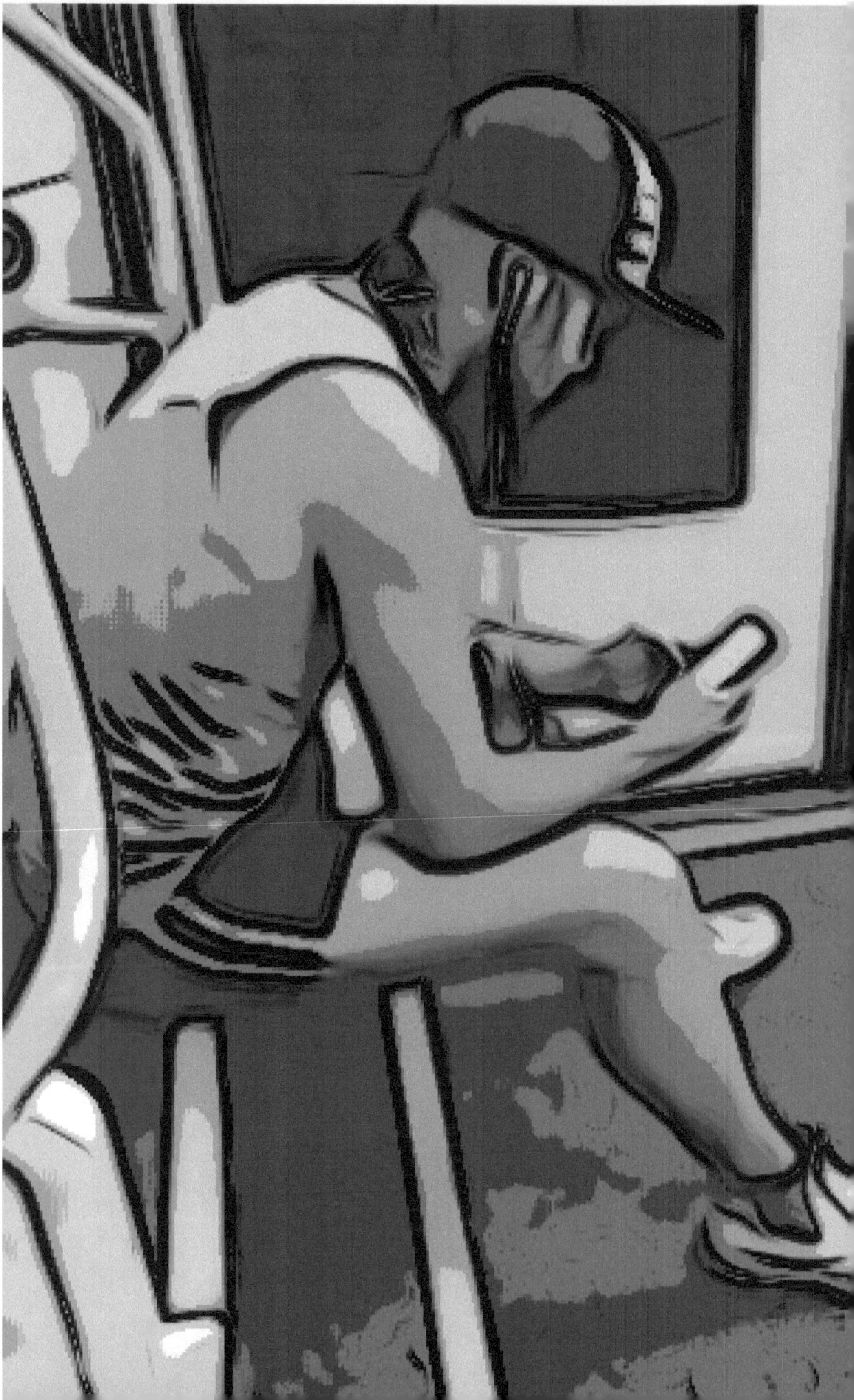

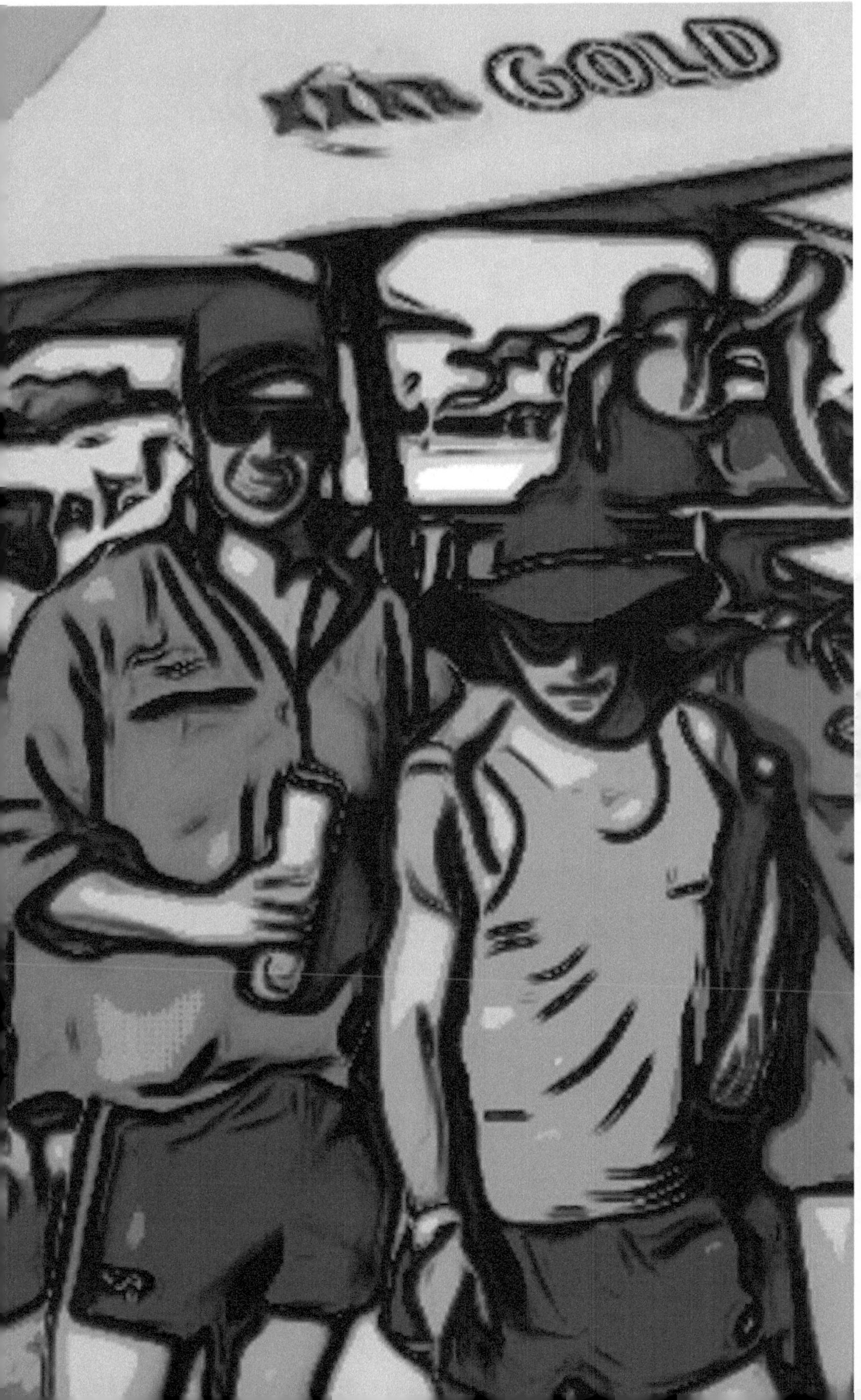
GOLD

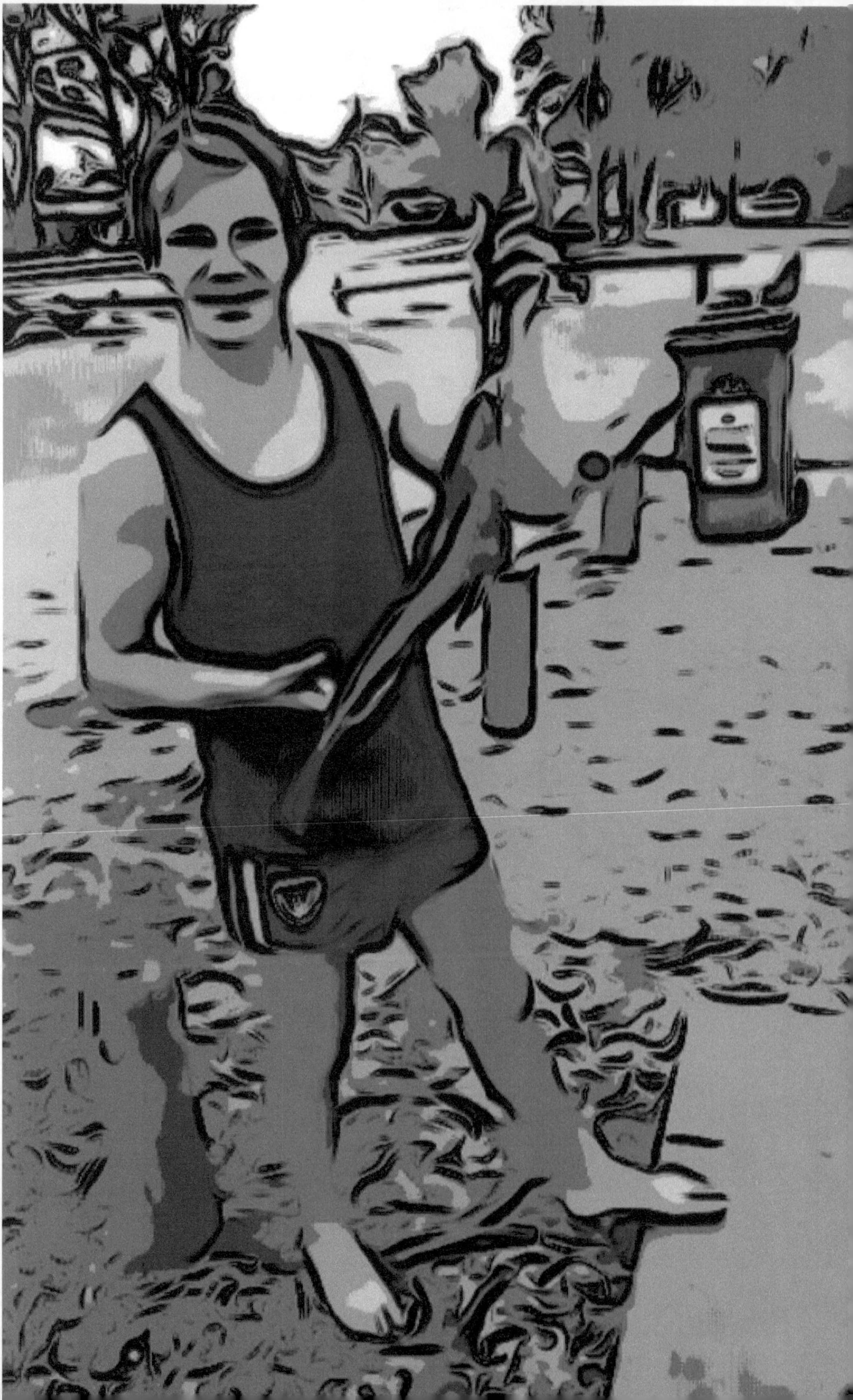

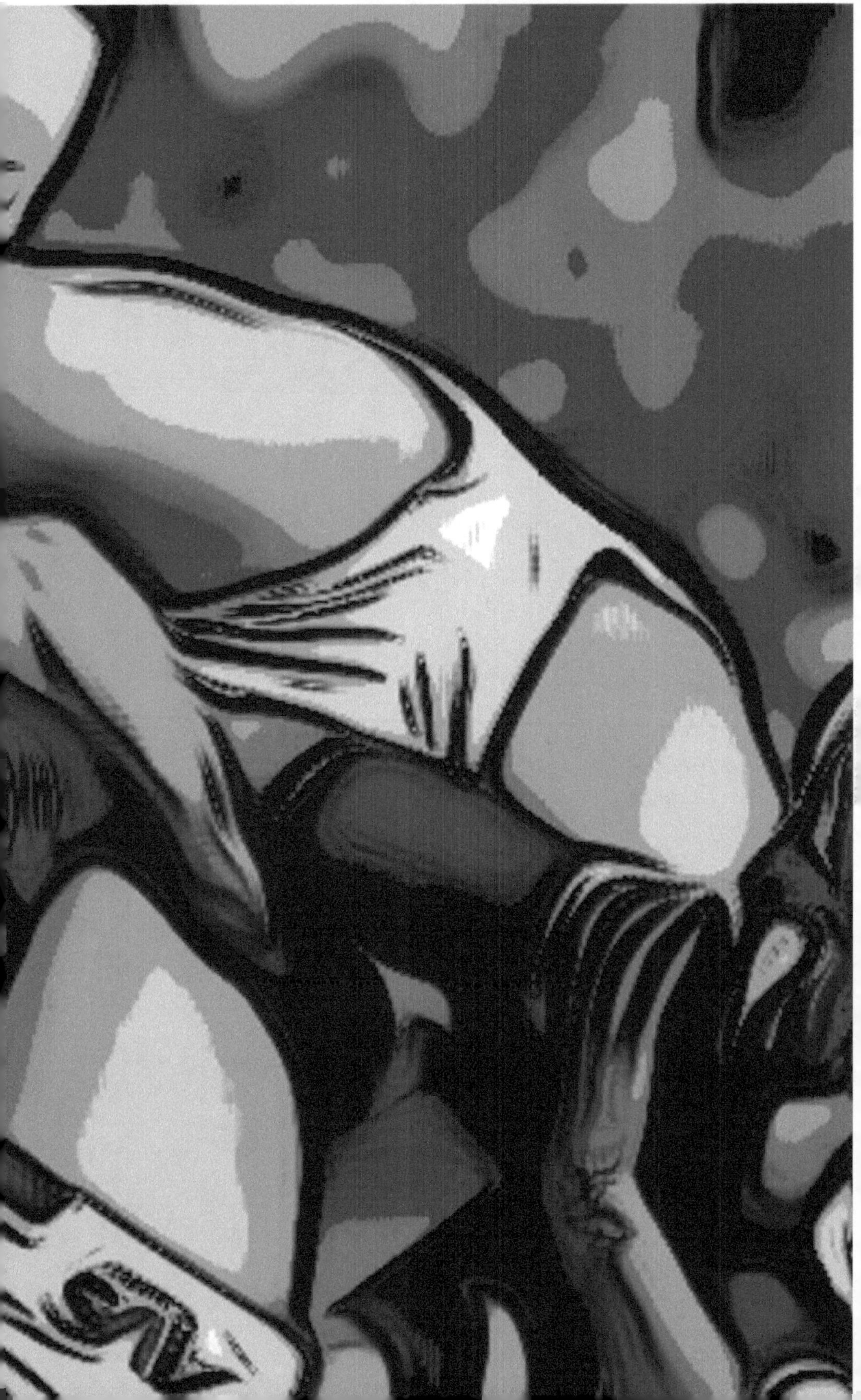

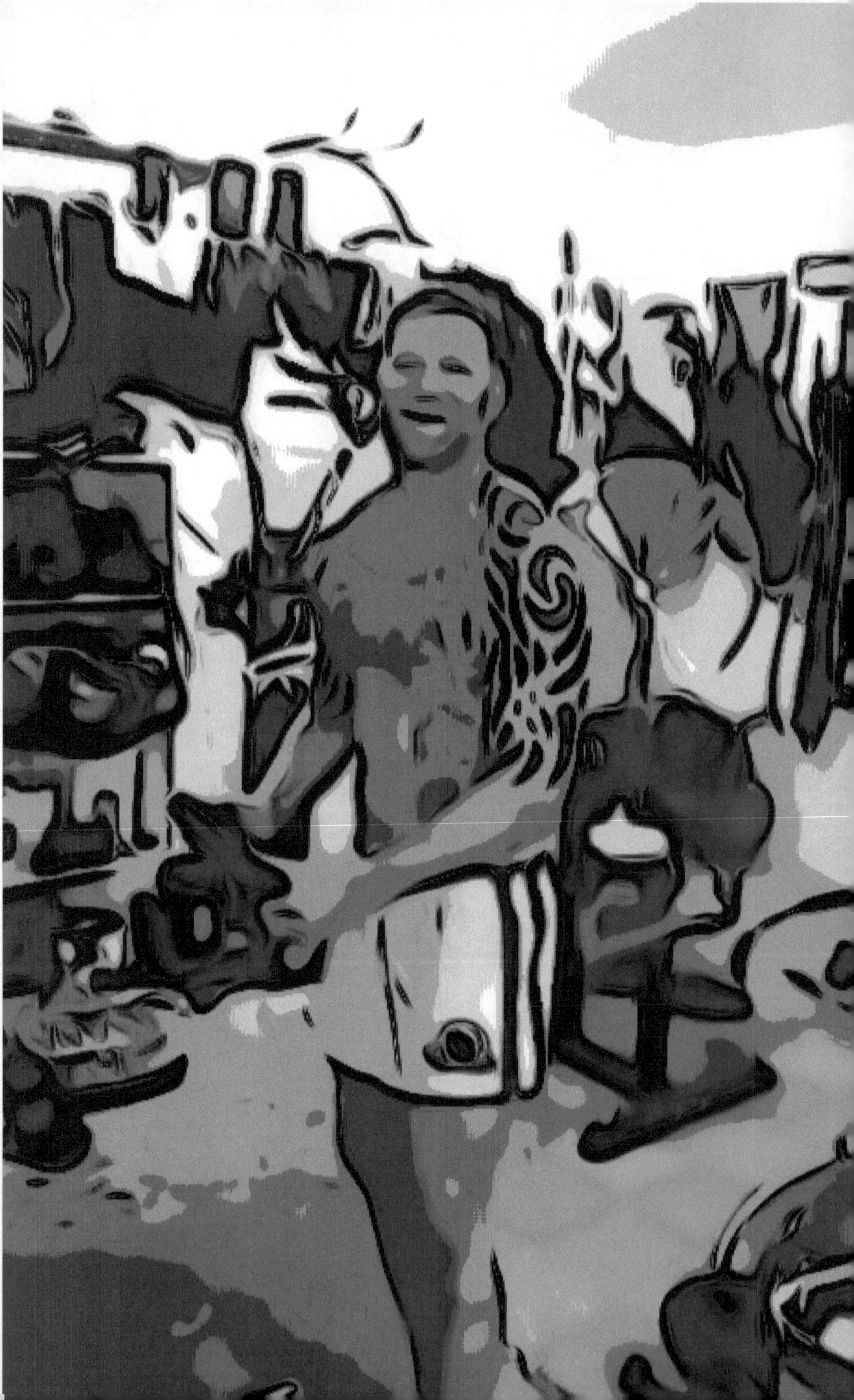

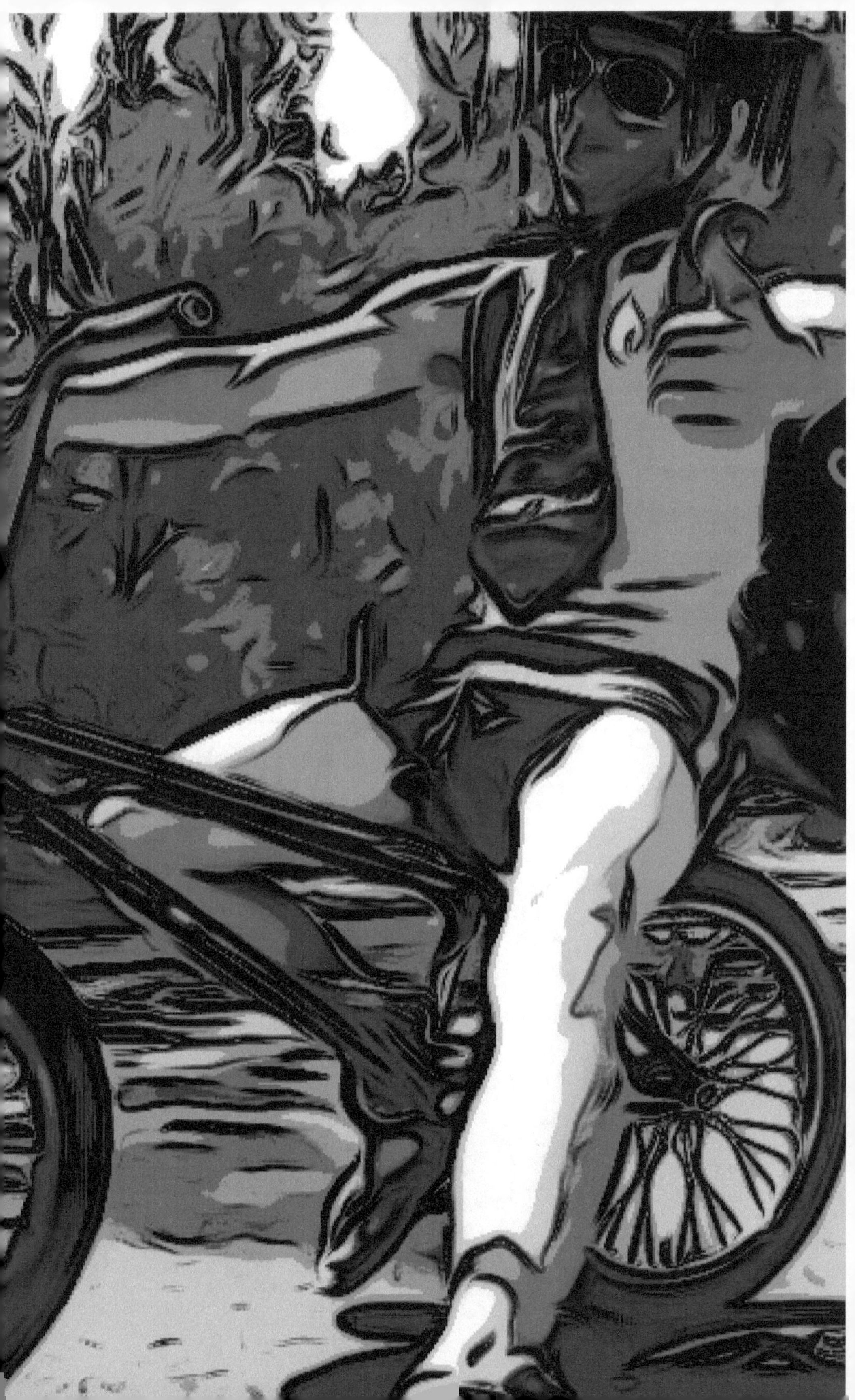

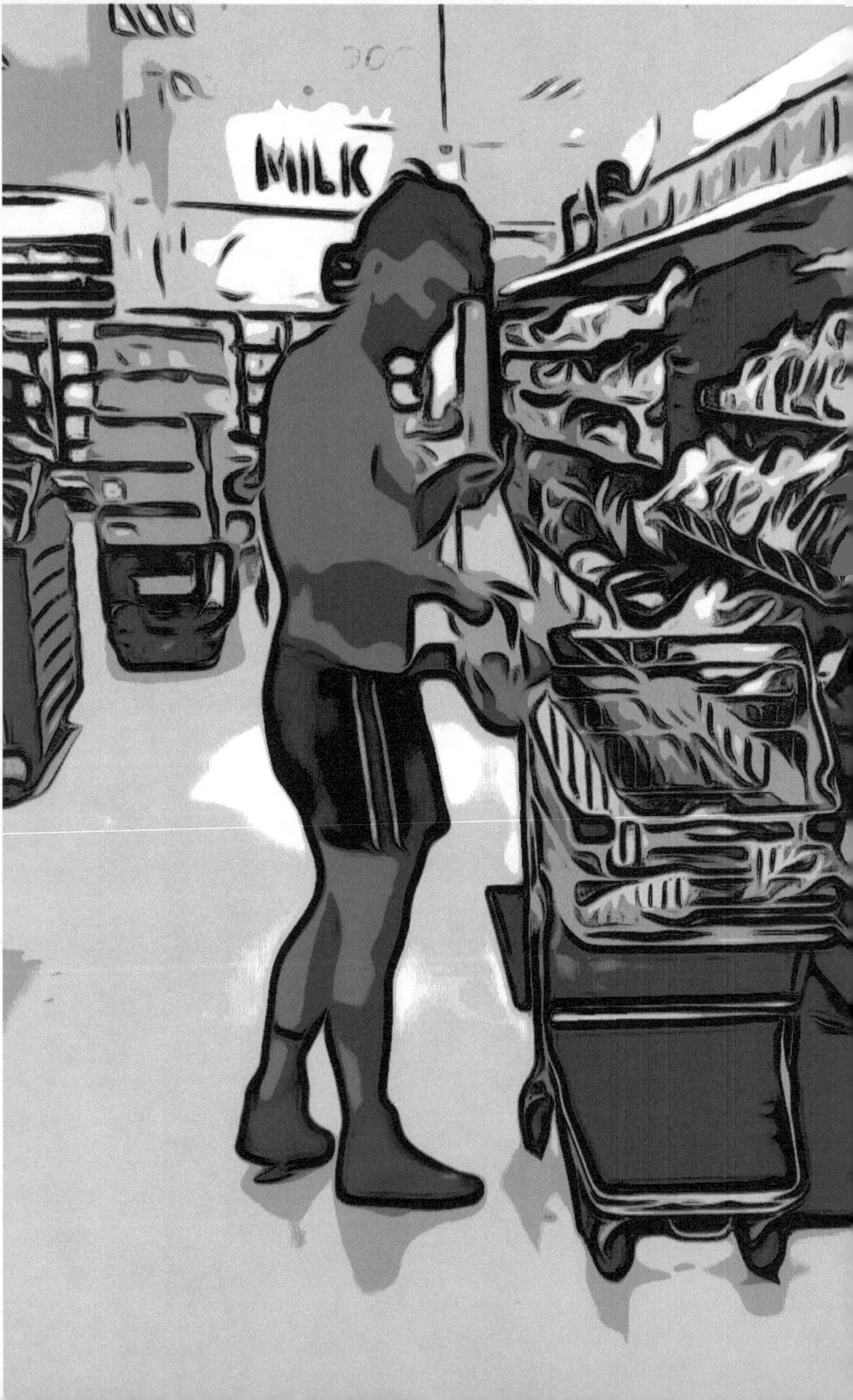
MILK

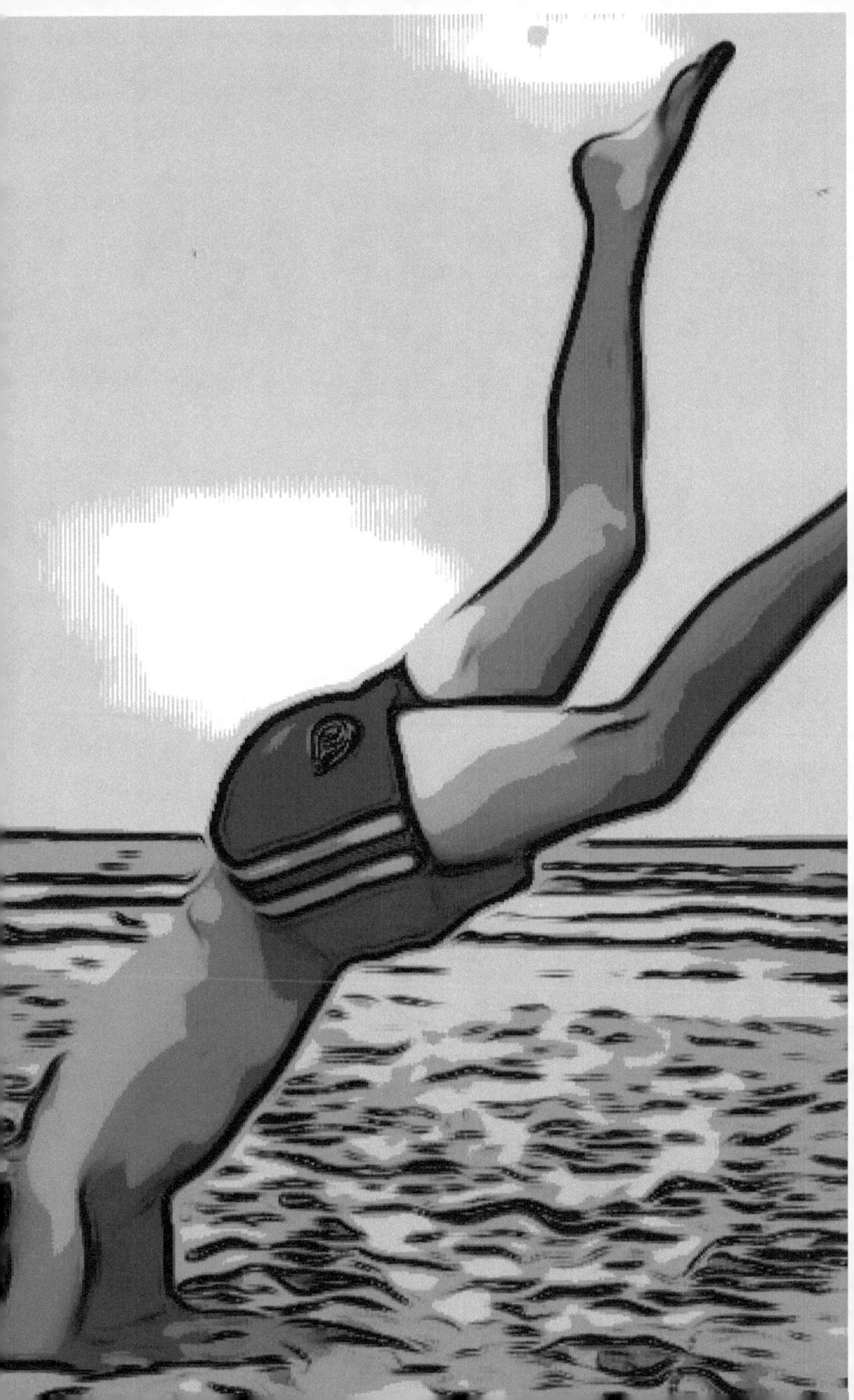

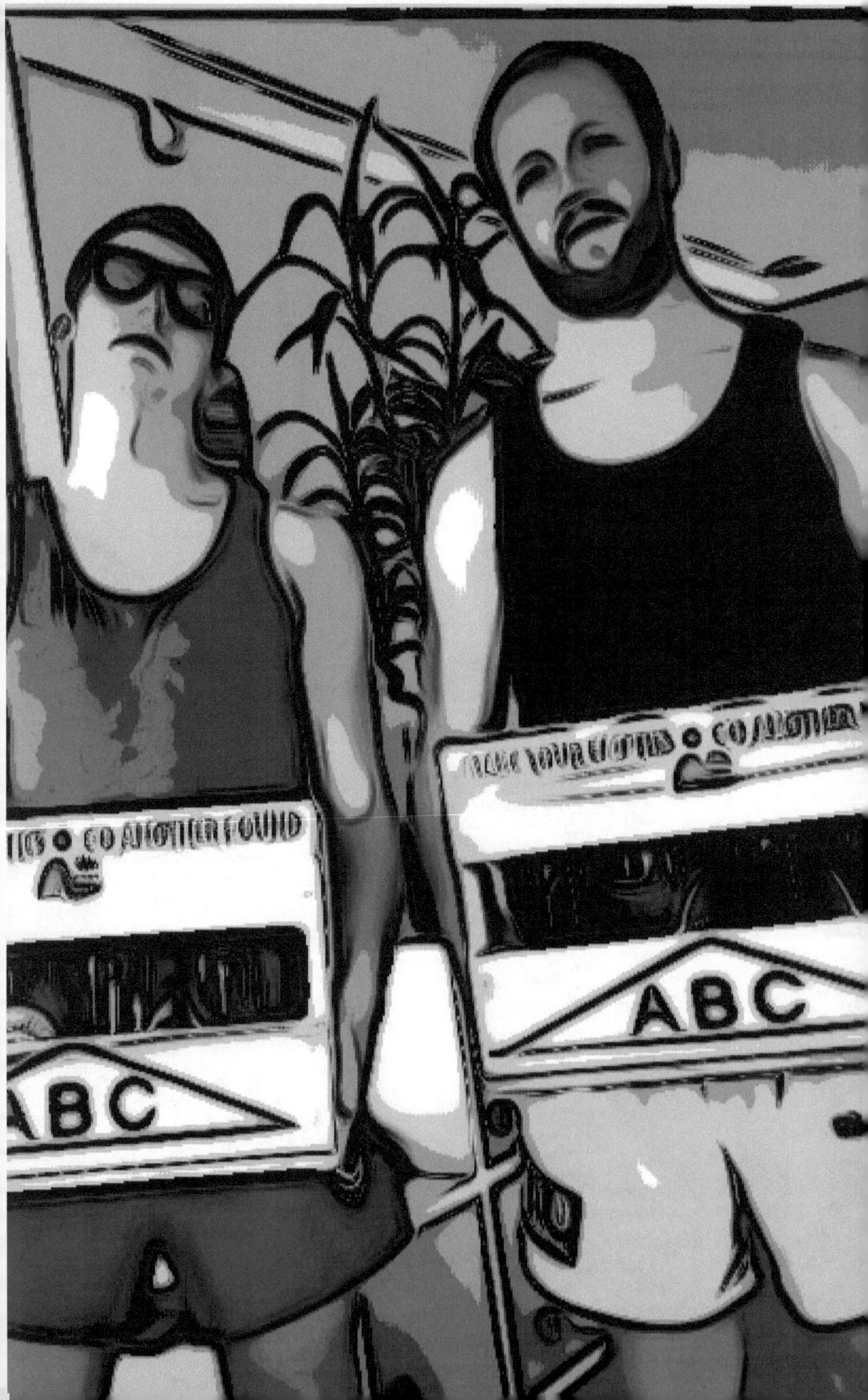
ABC
ABC

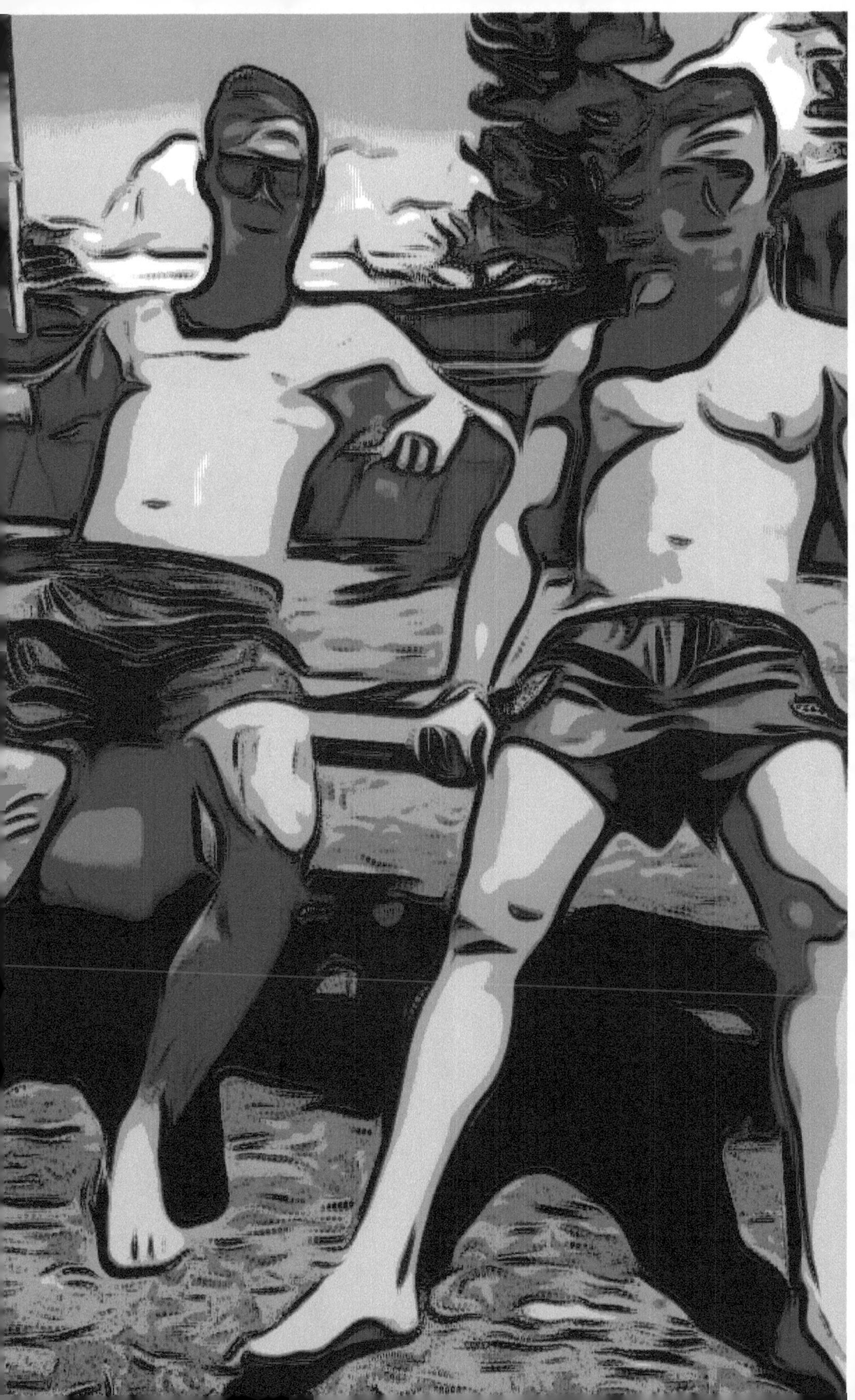

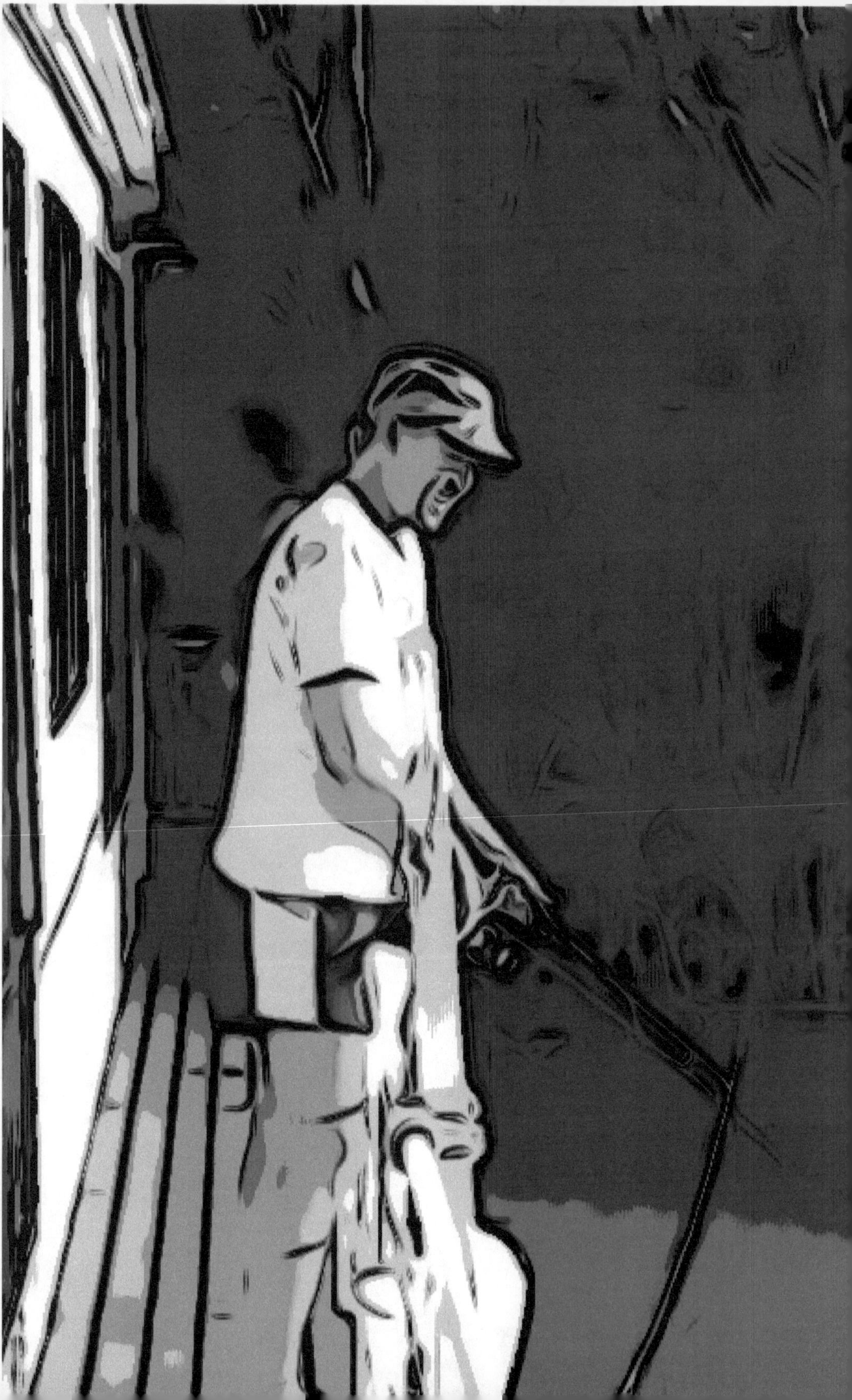

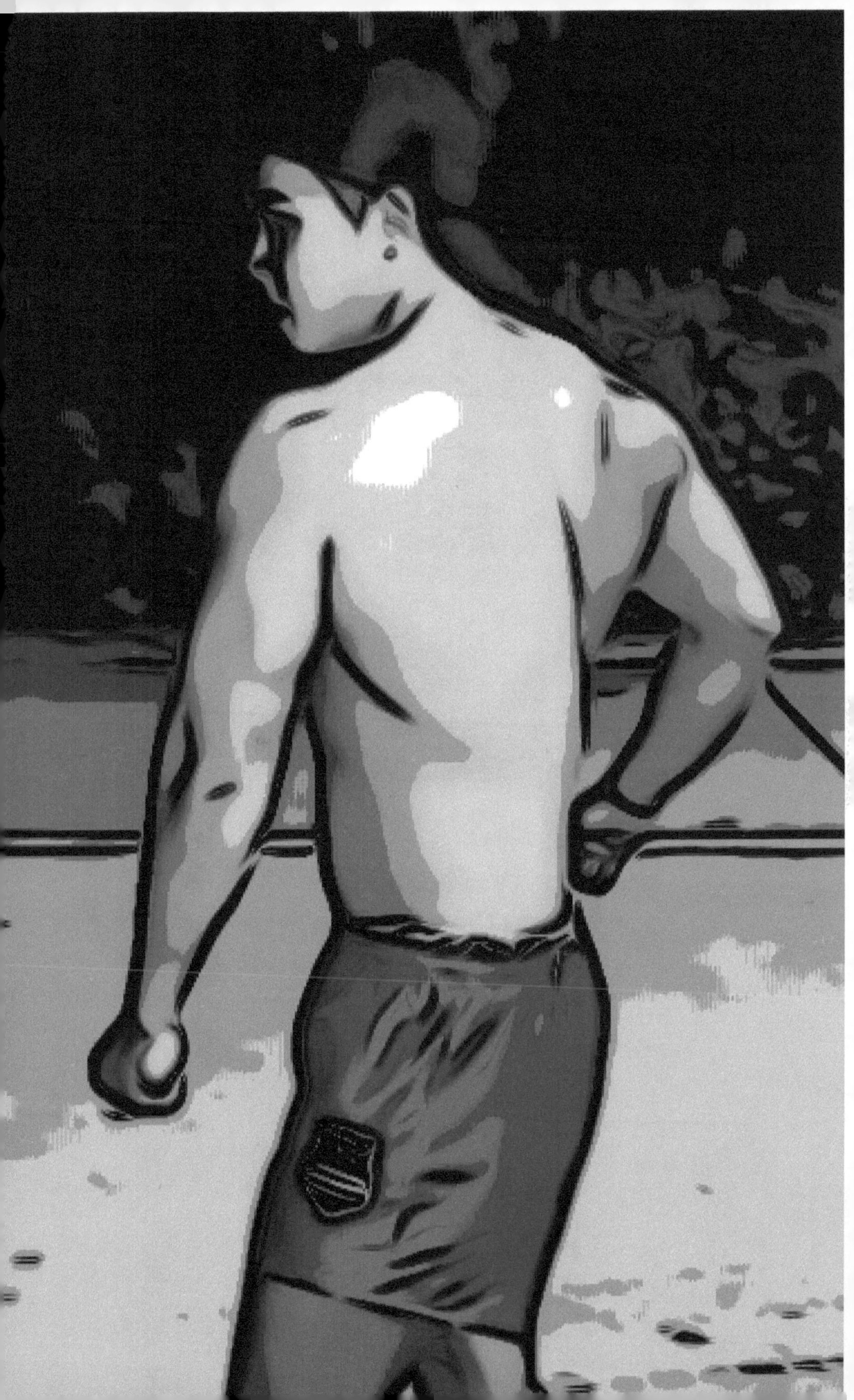

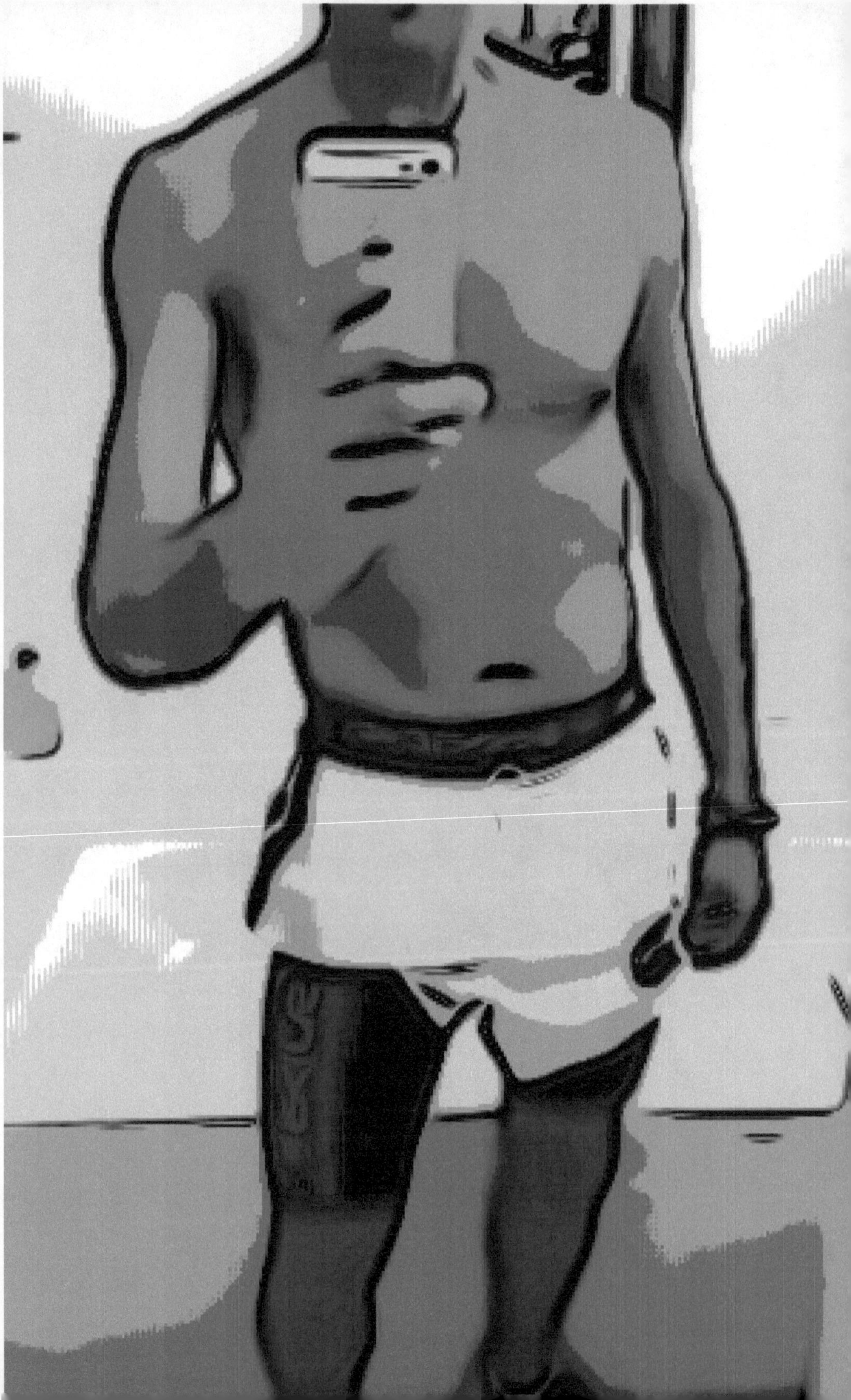

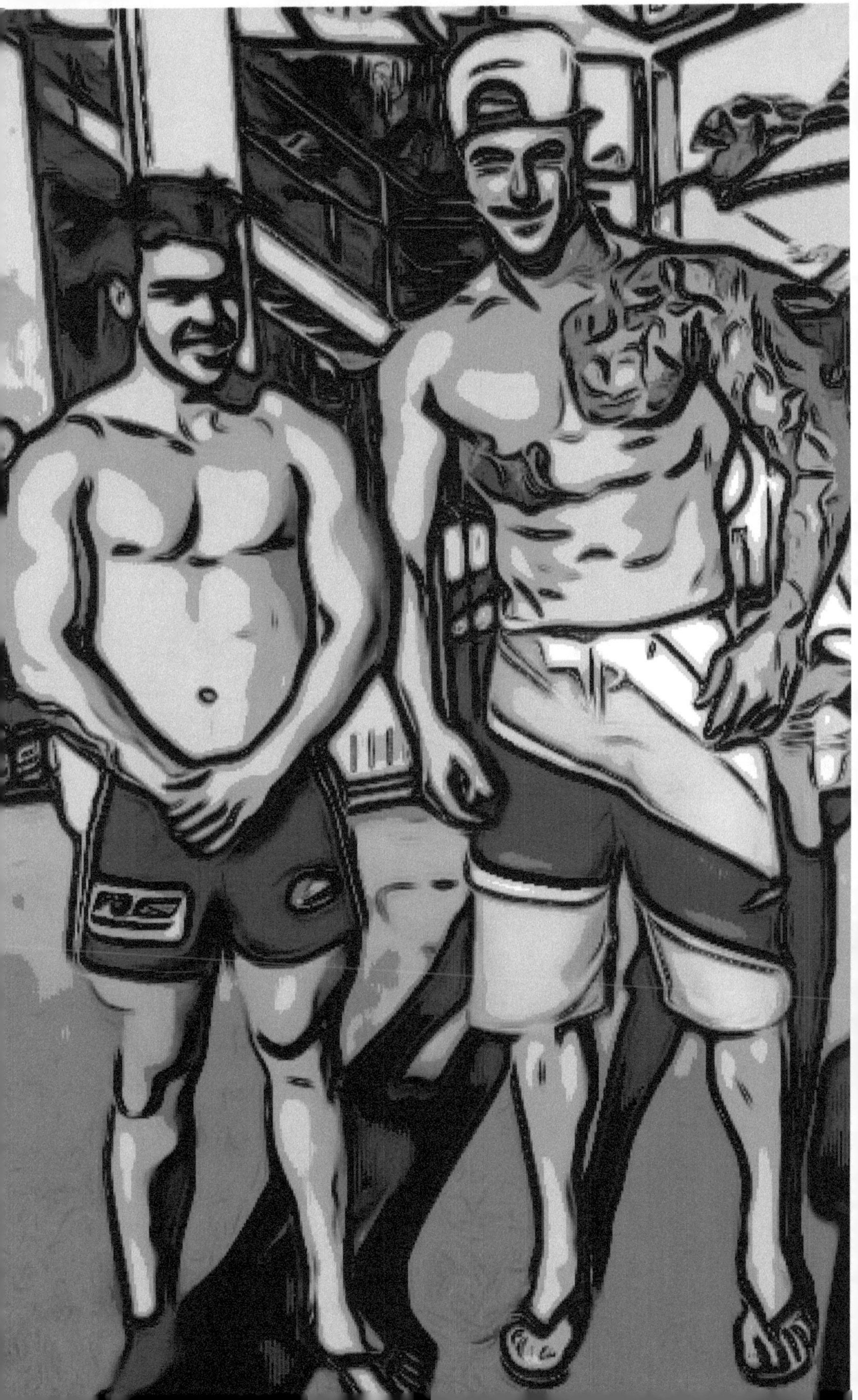

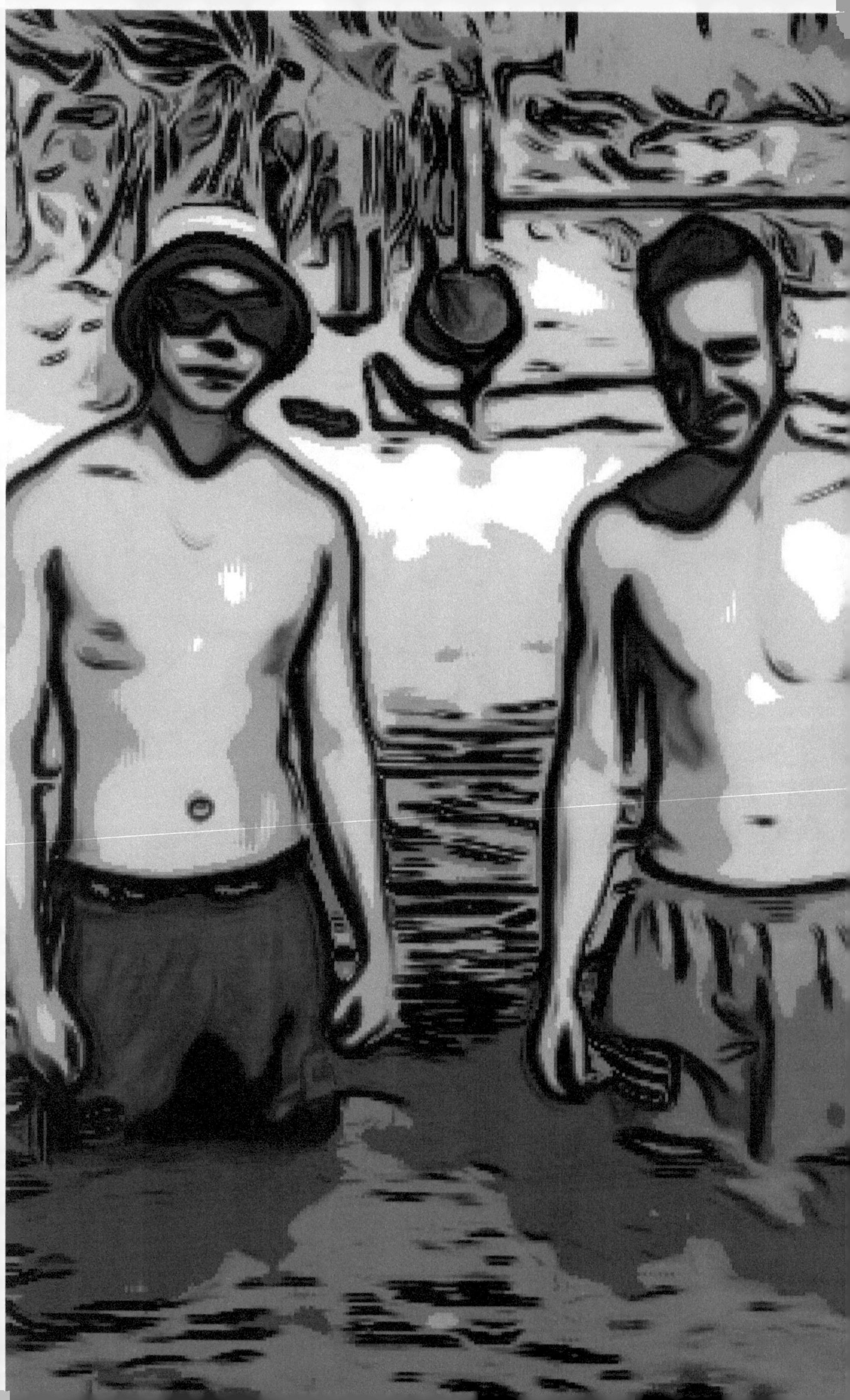

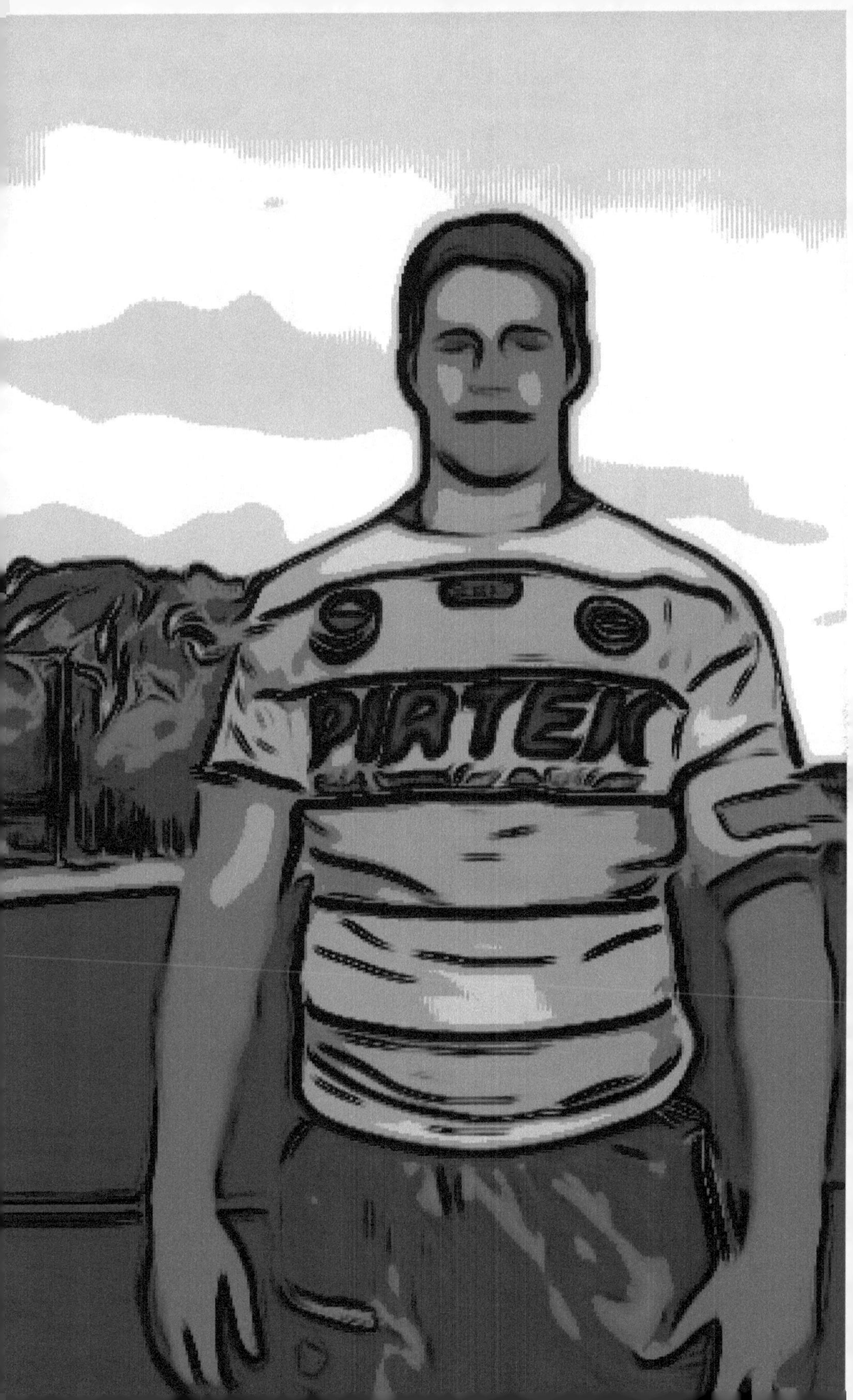
PIRTEK

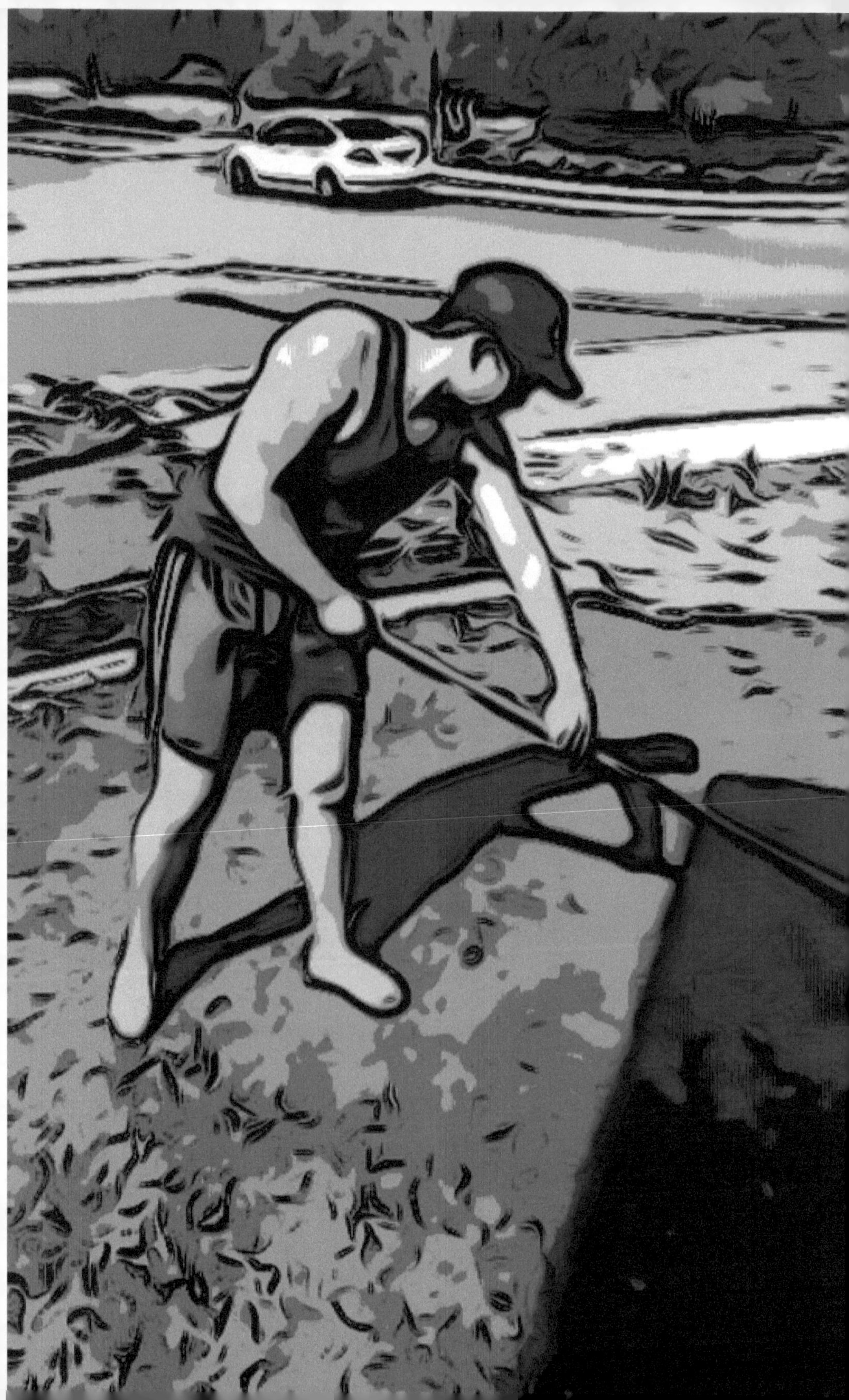

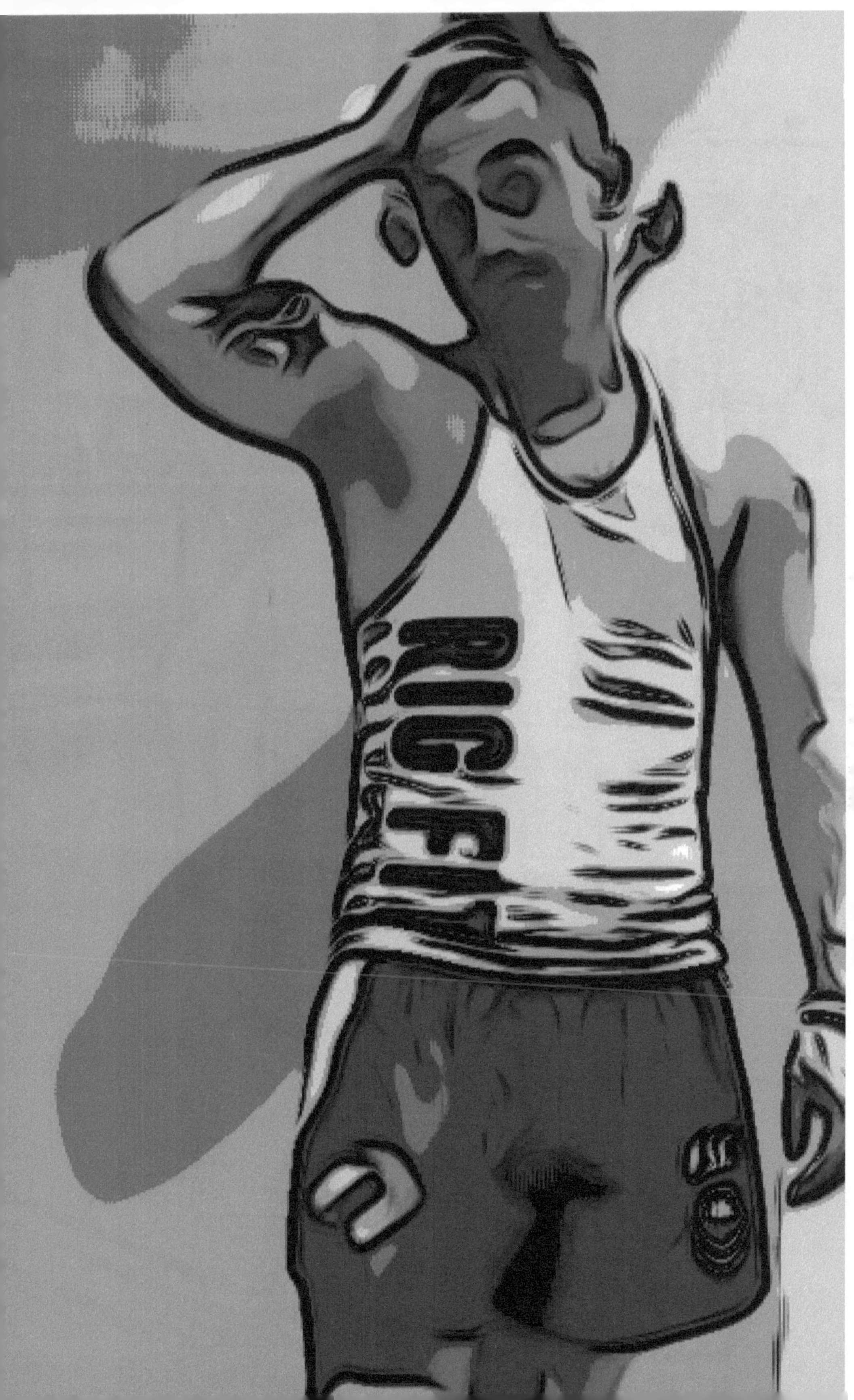

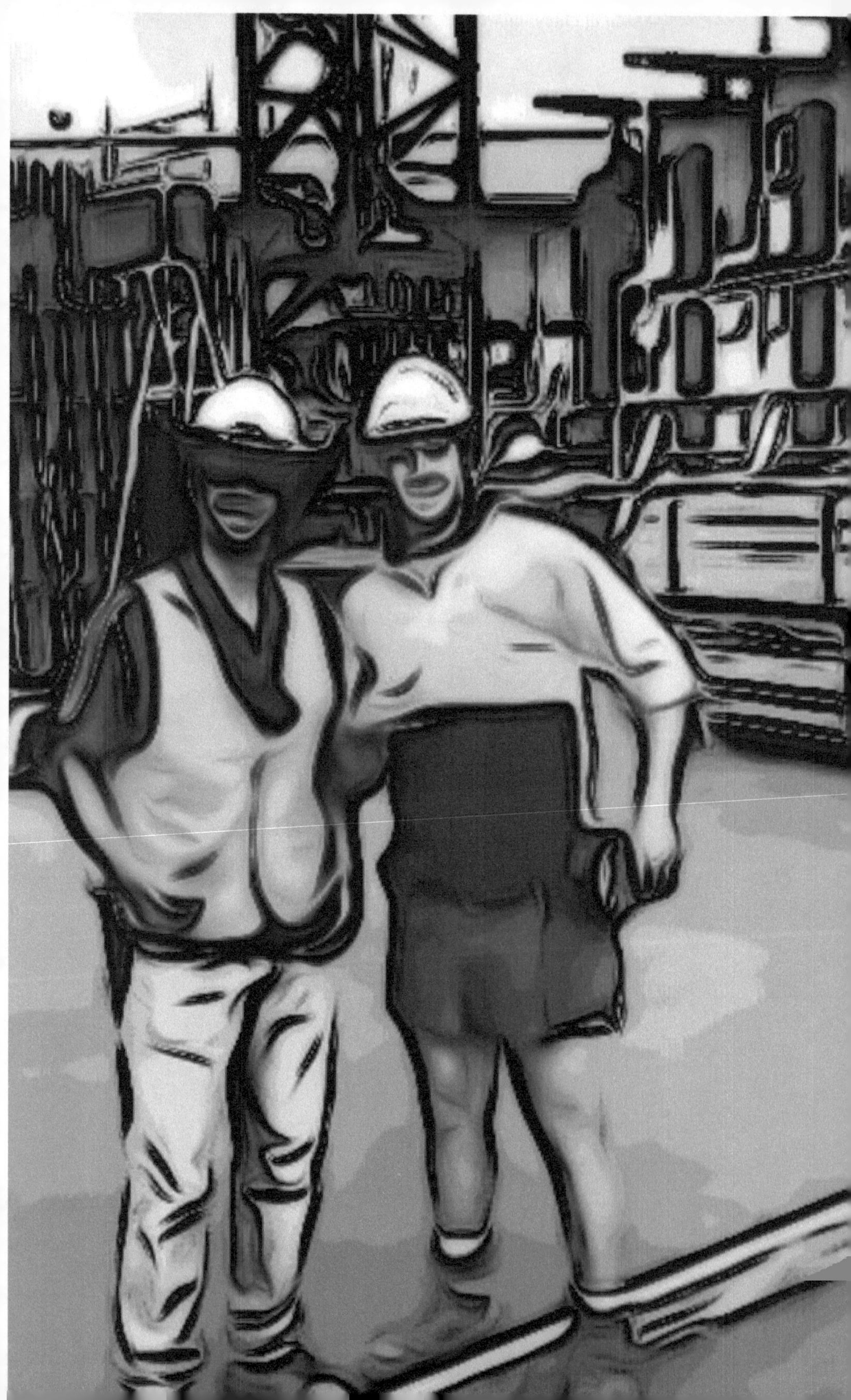

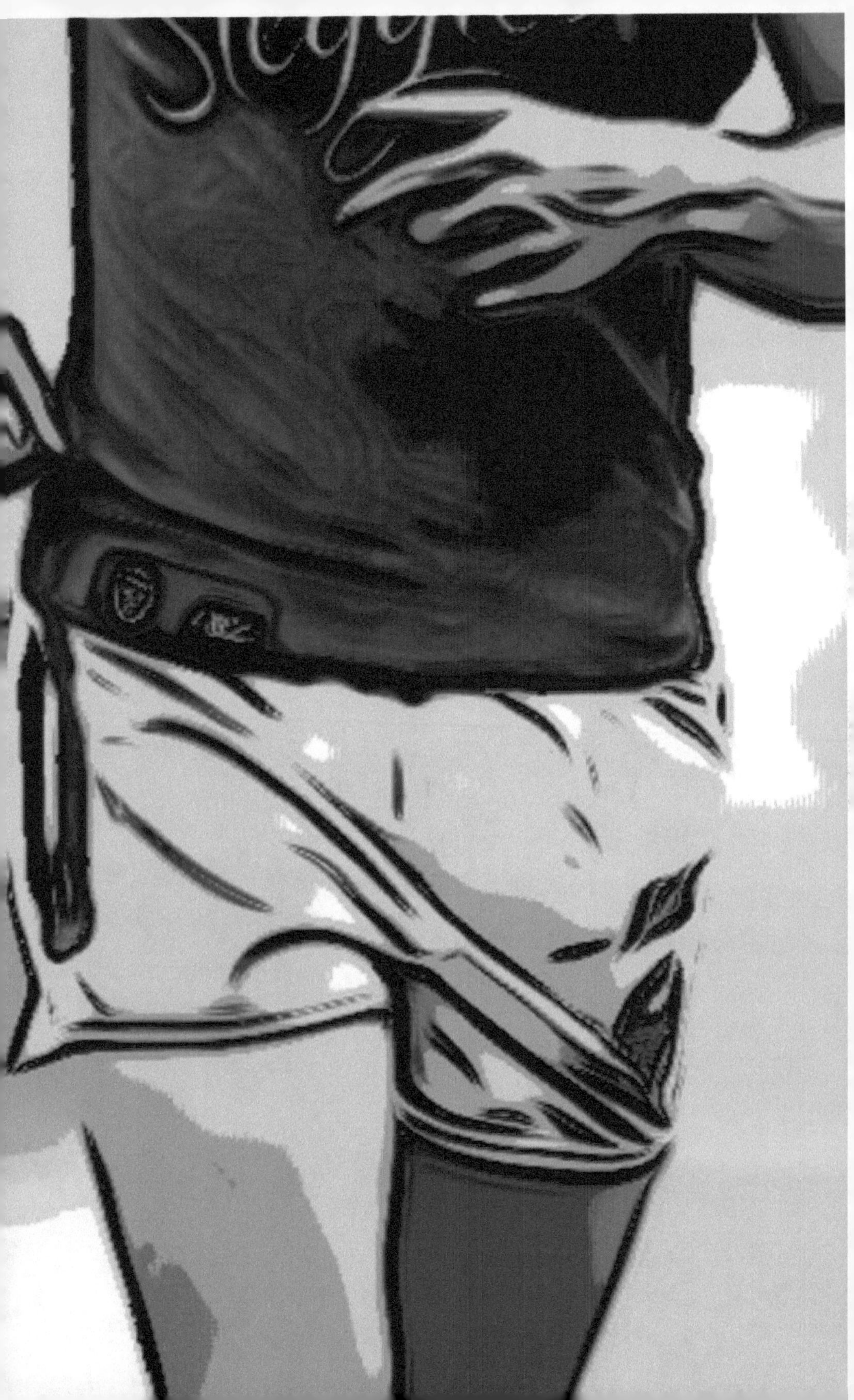

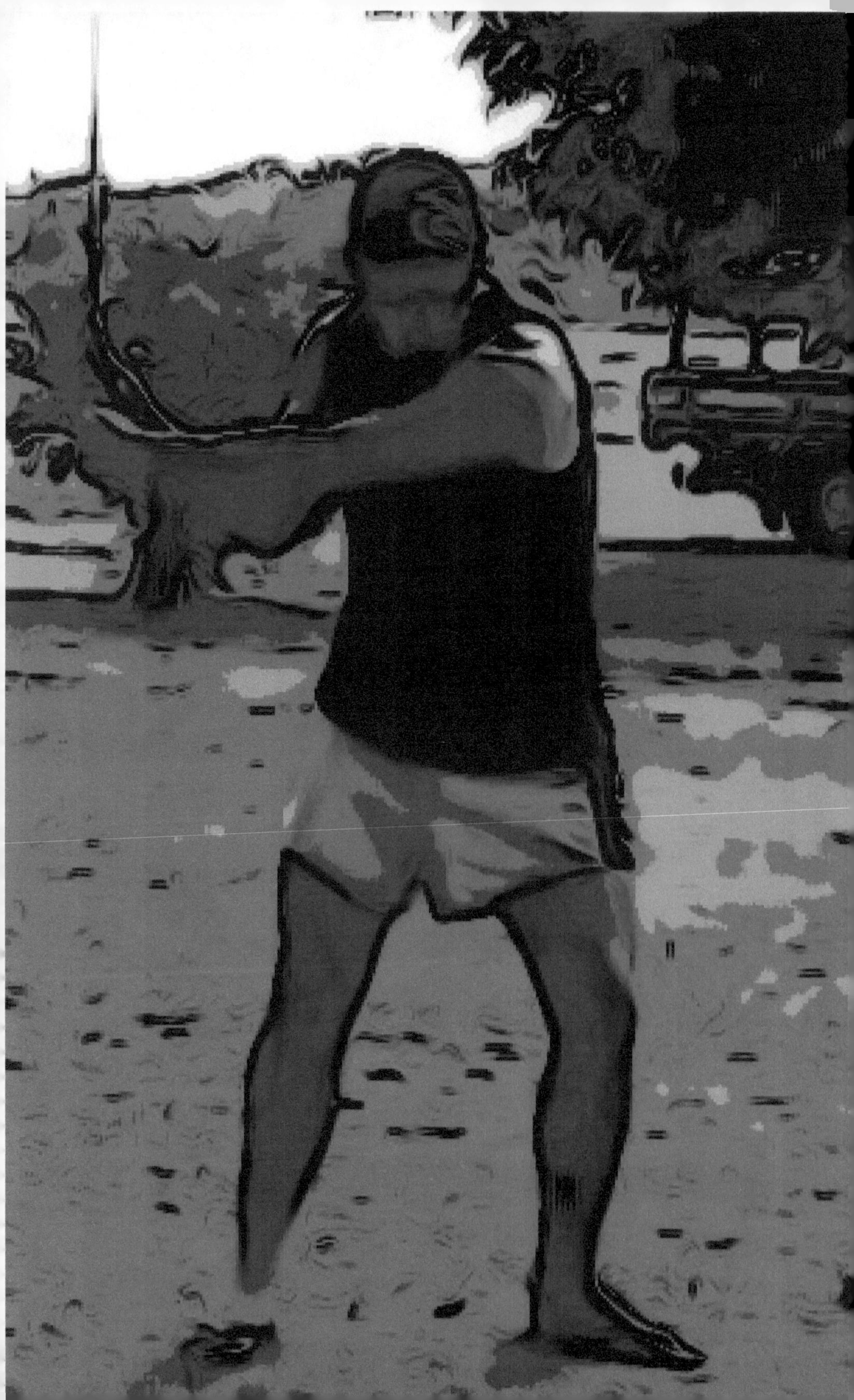

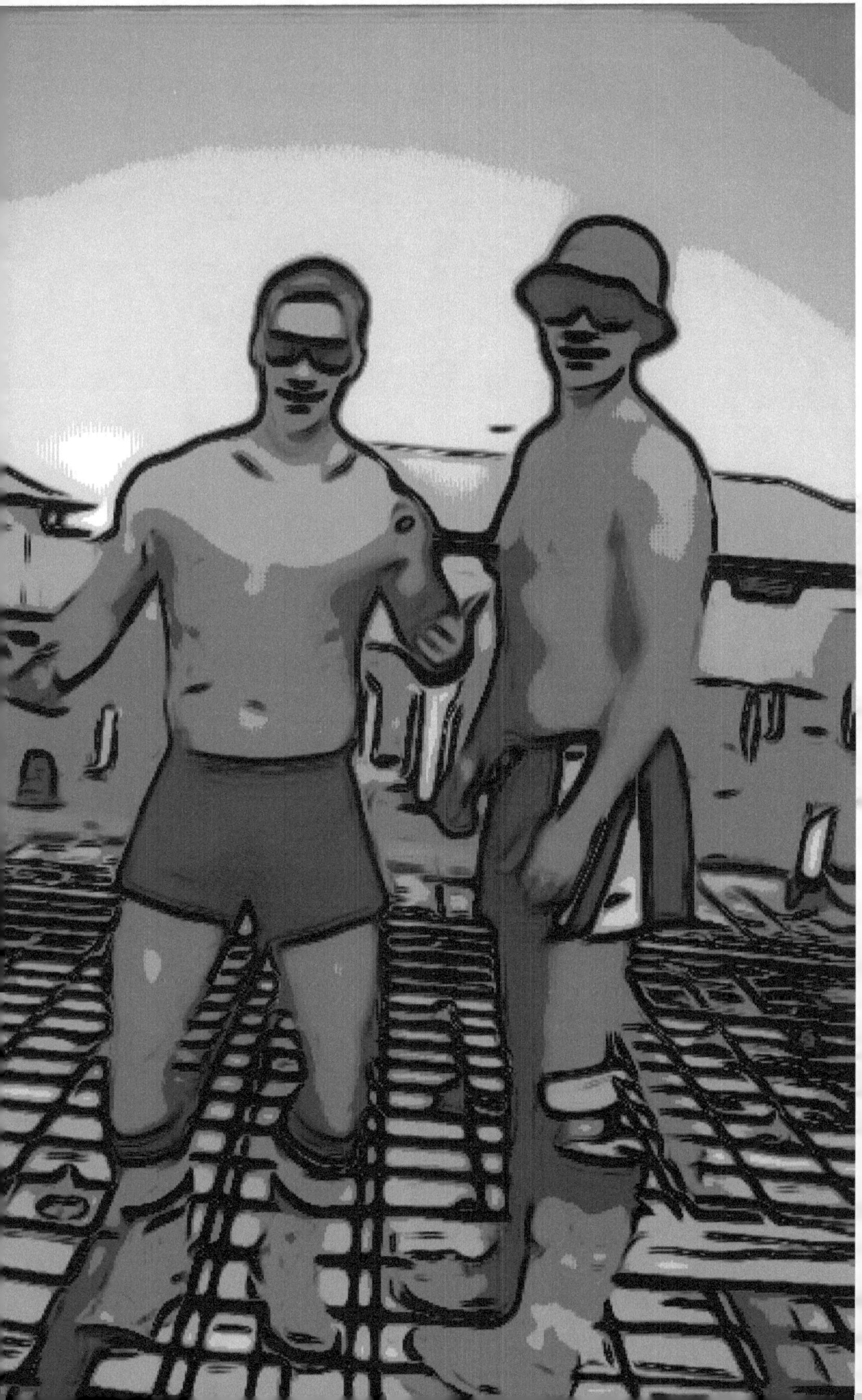

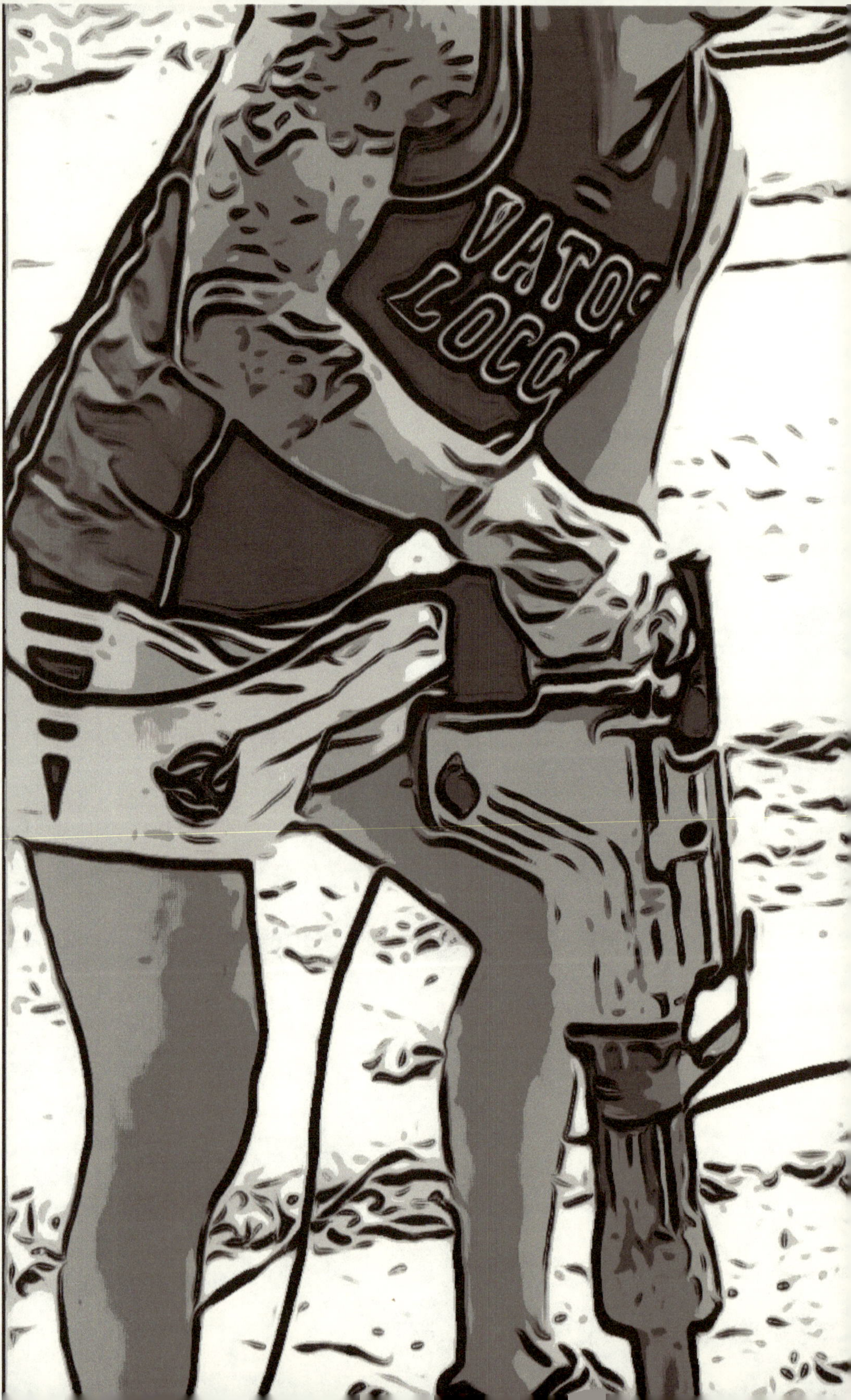
VATOS
LOCO

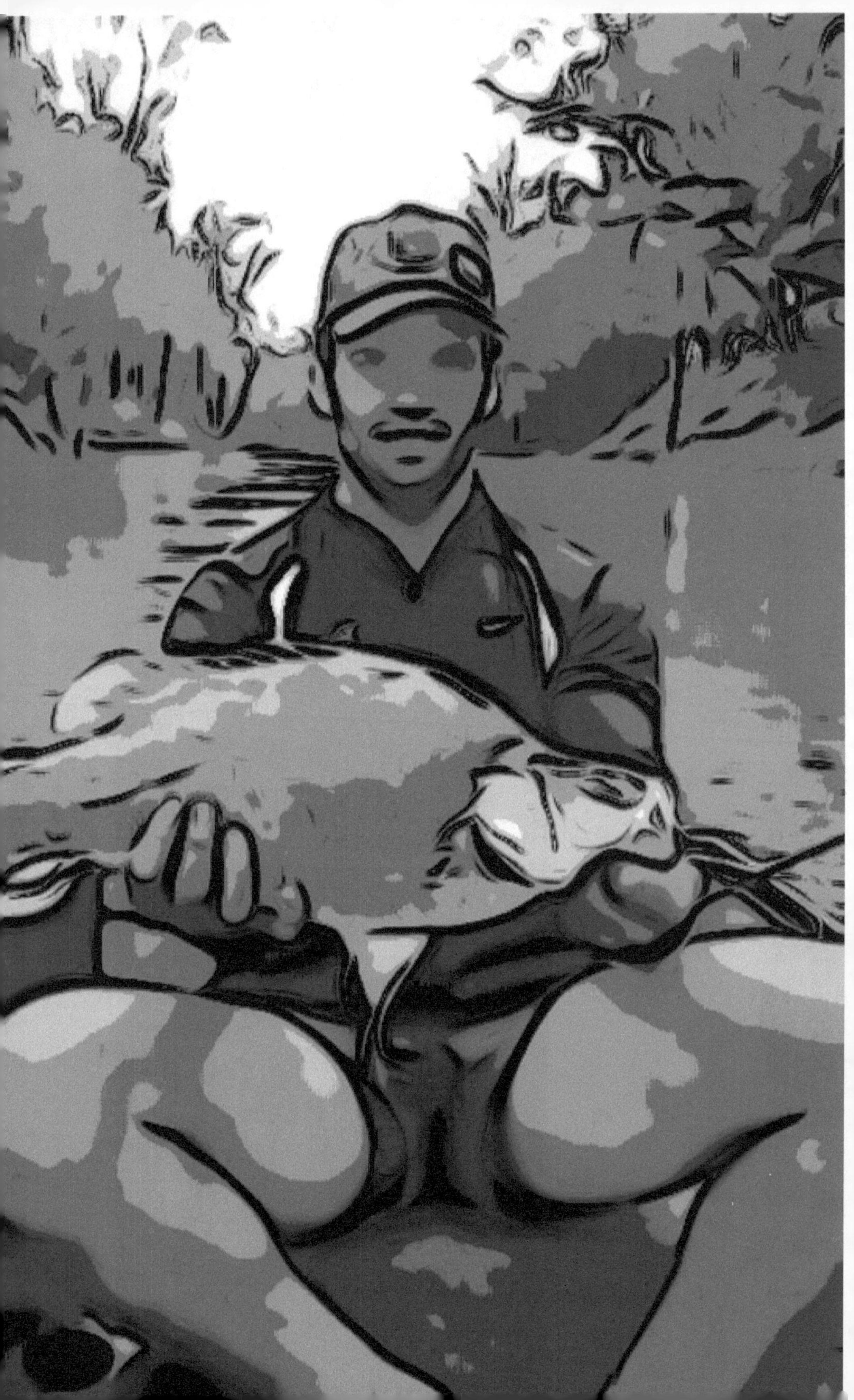

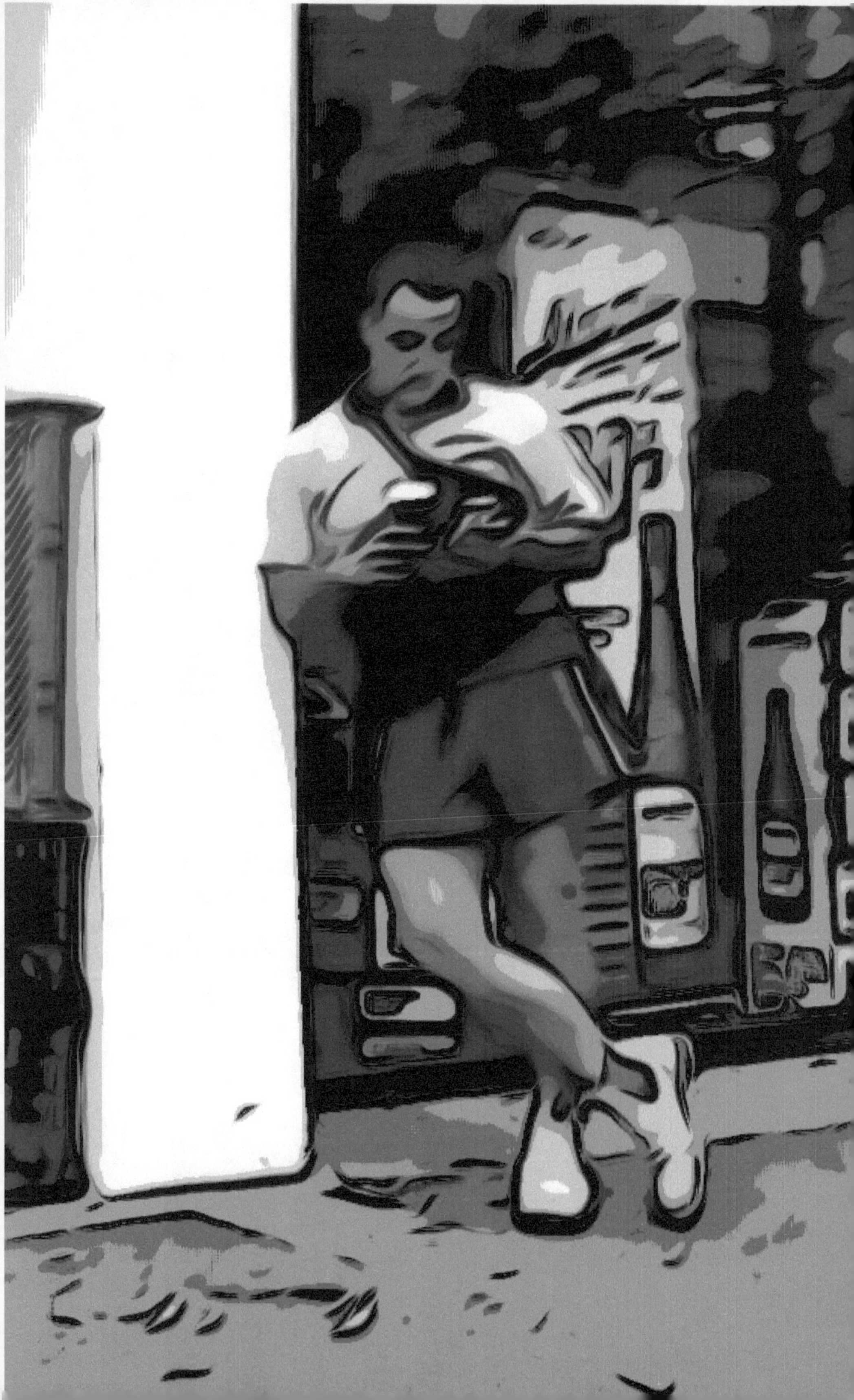

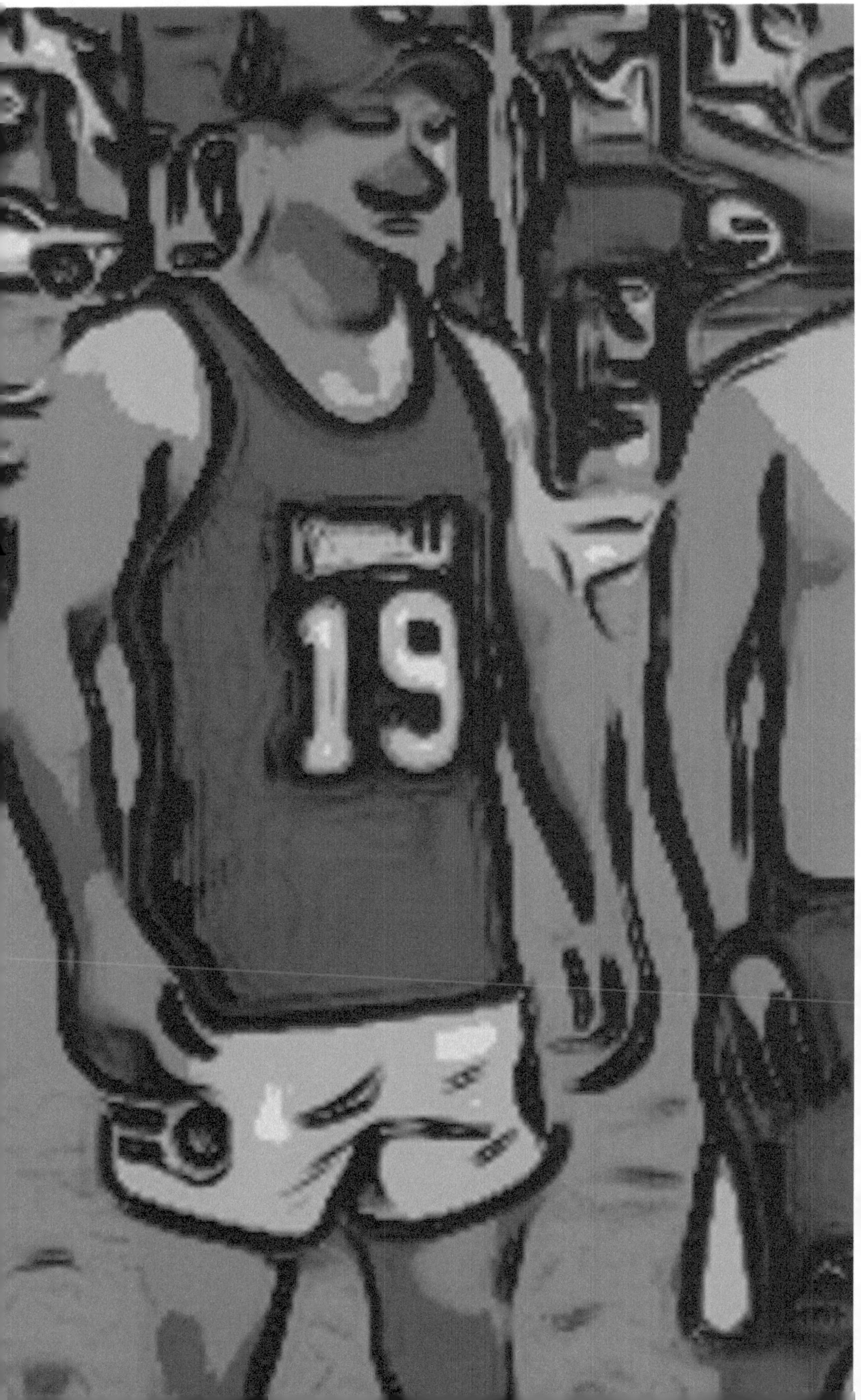
19

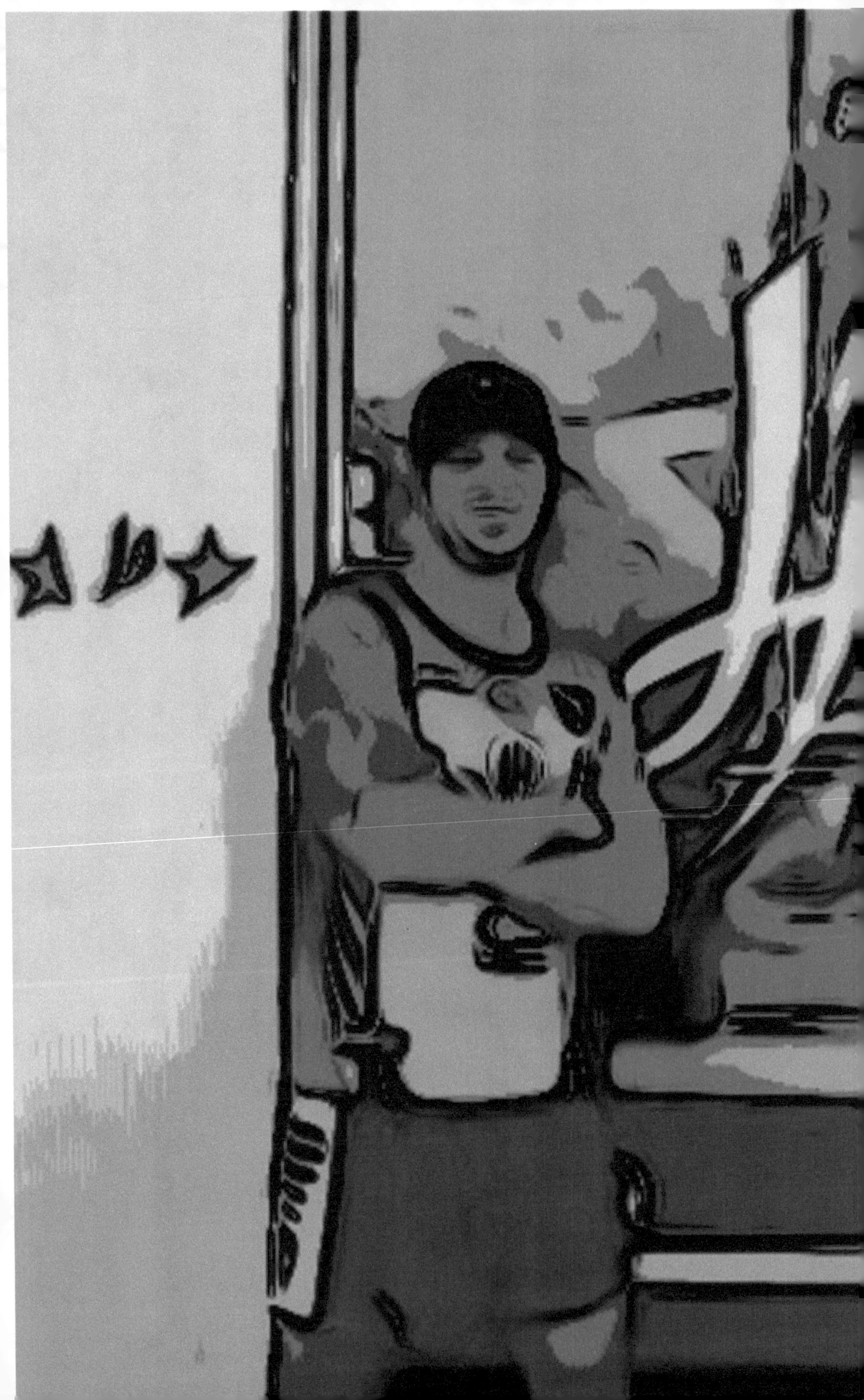

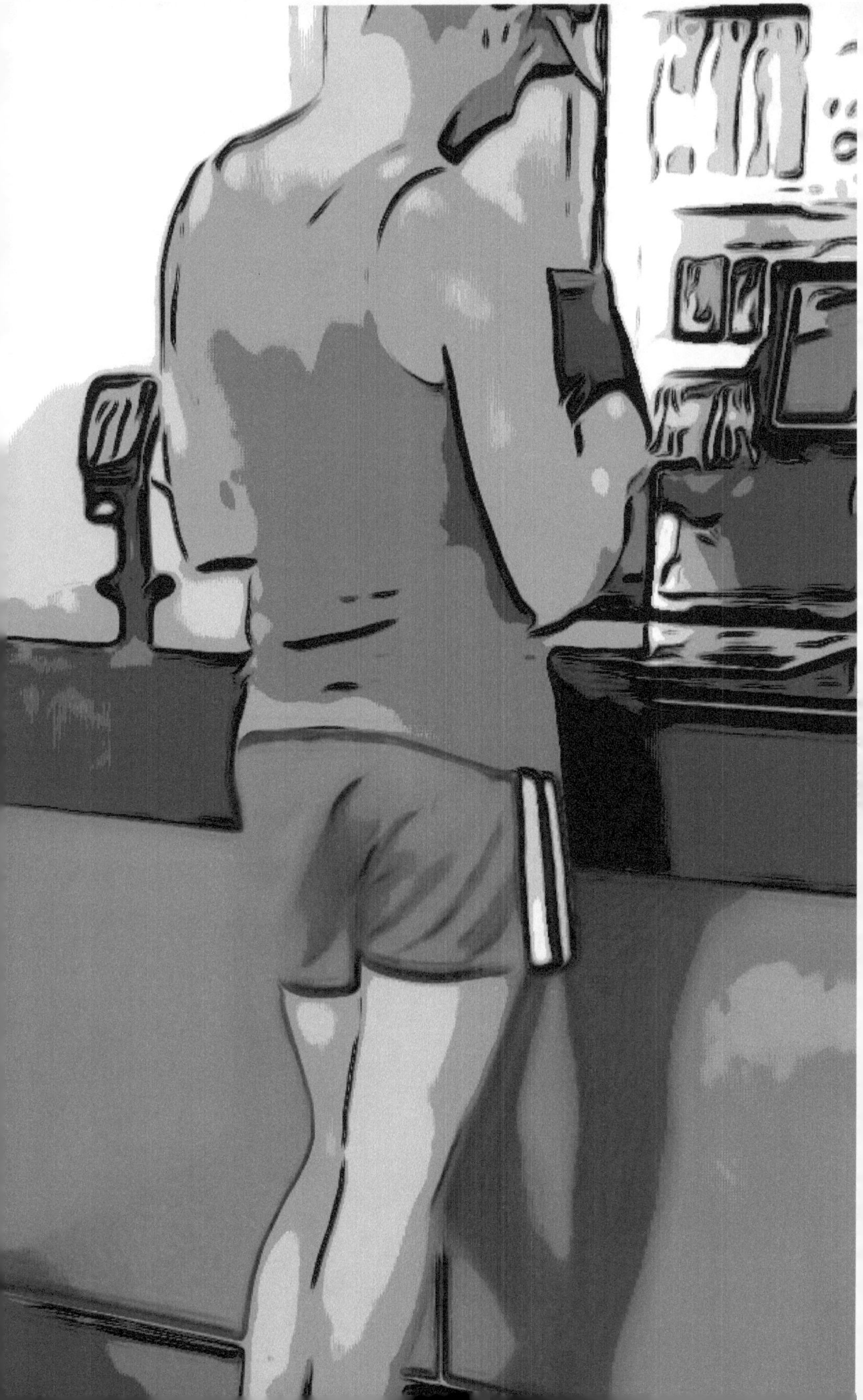

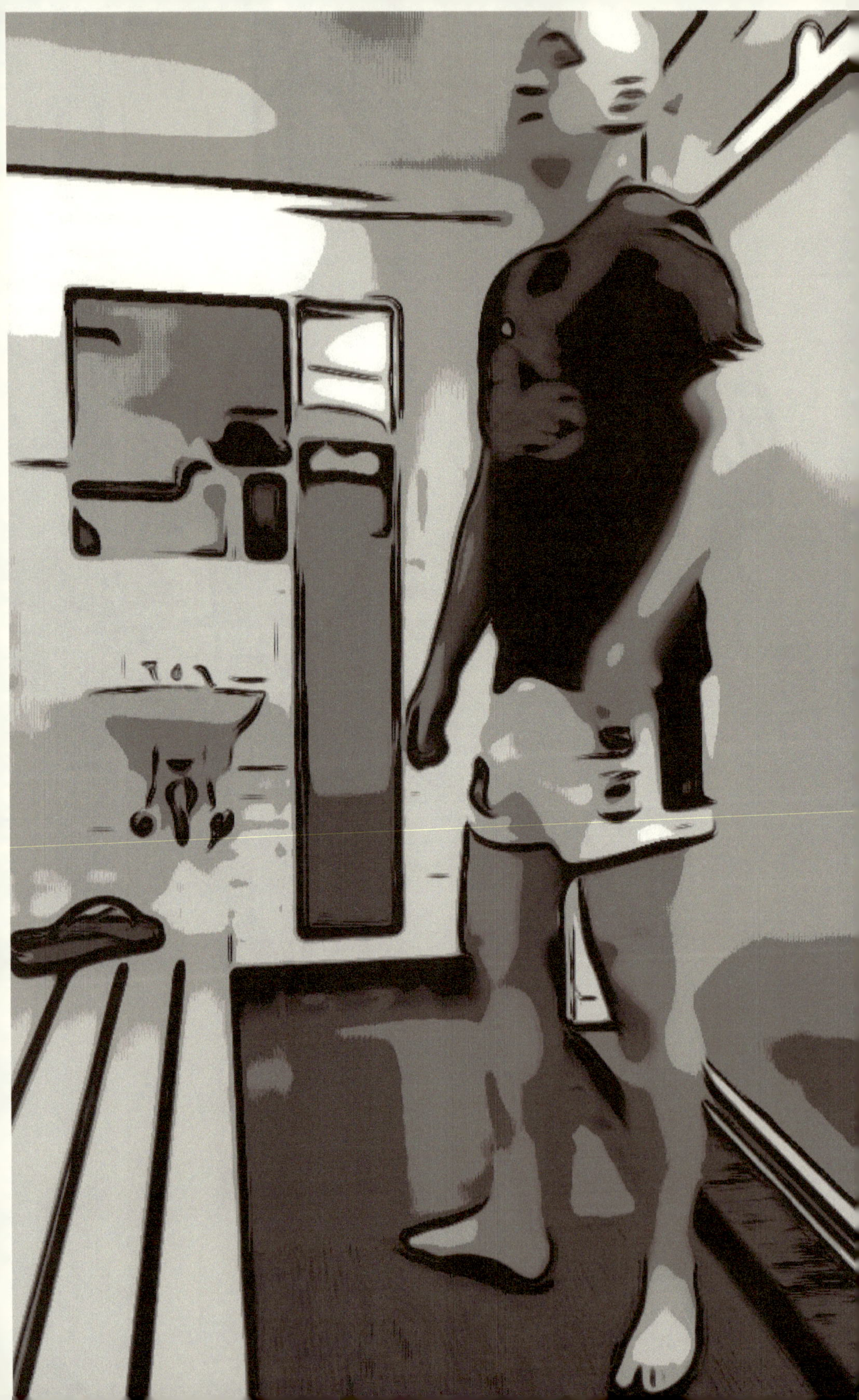

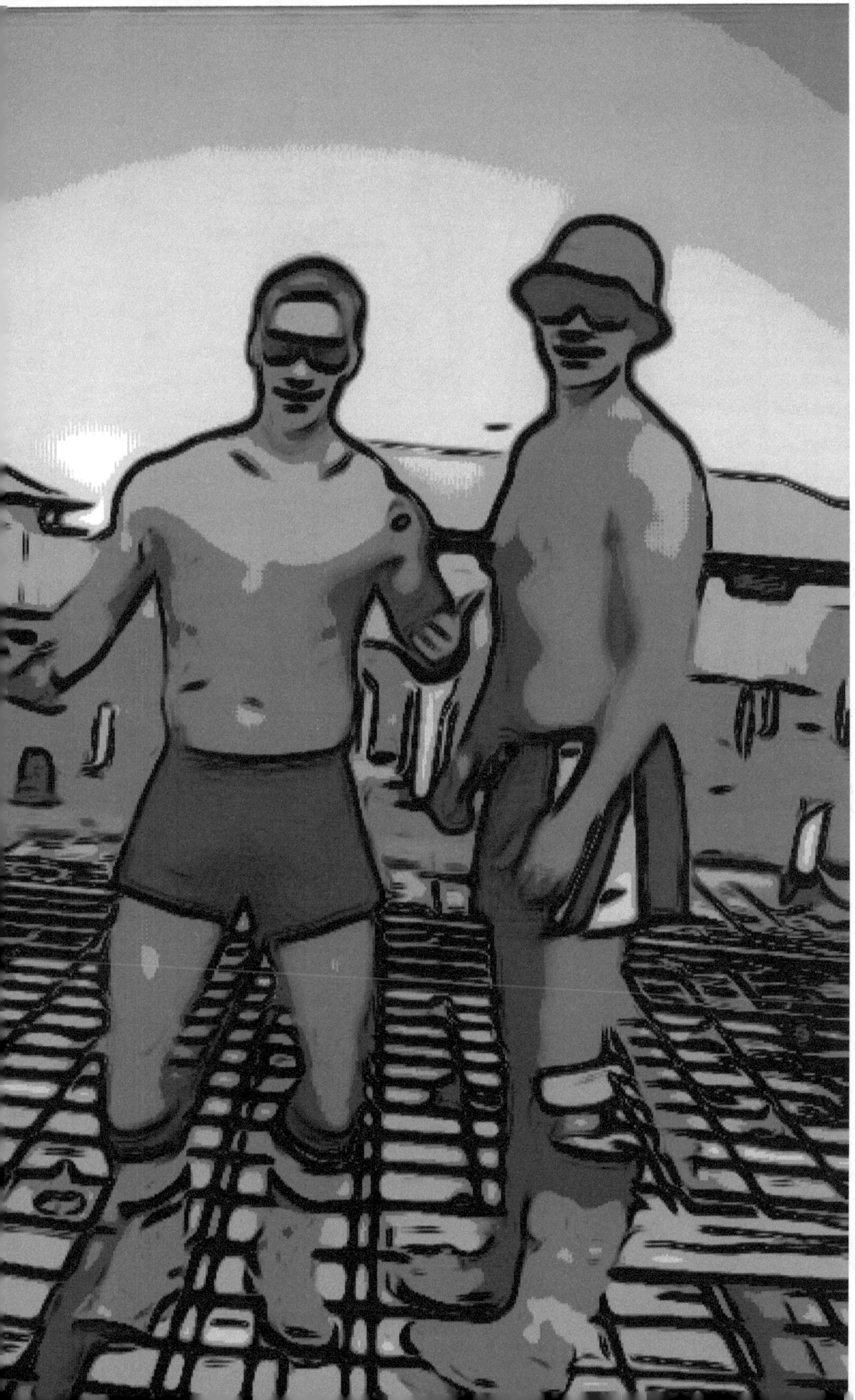

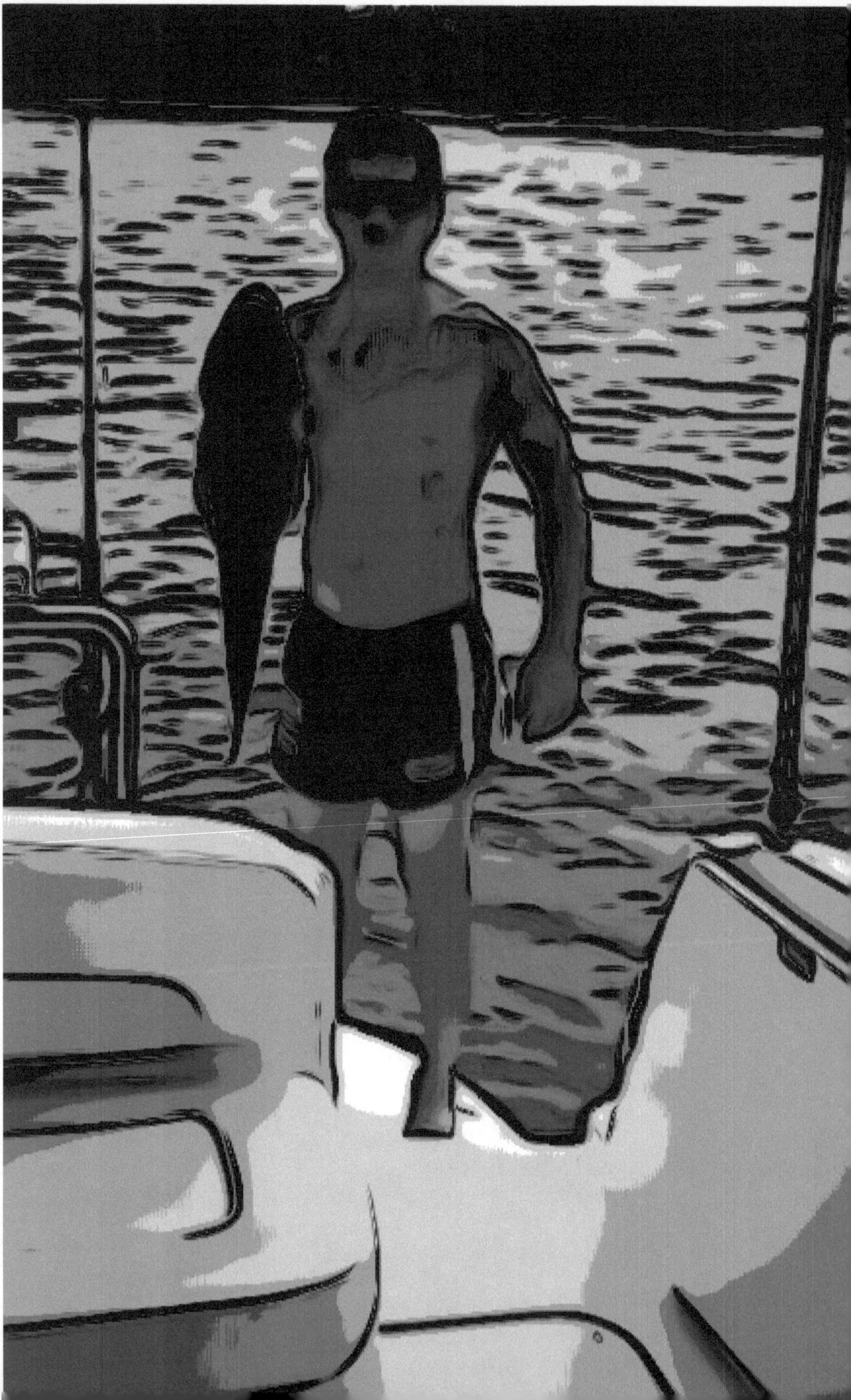

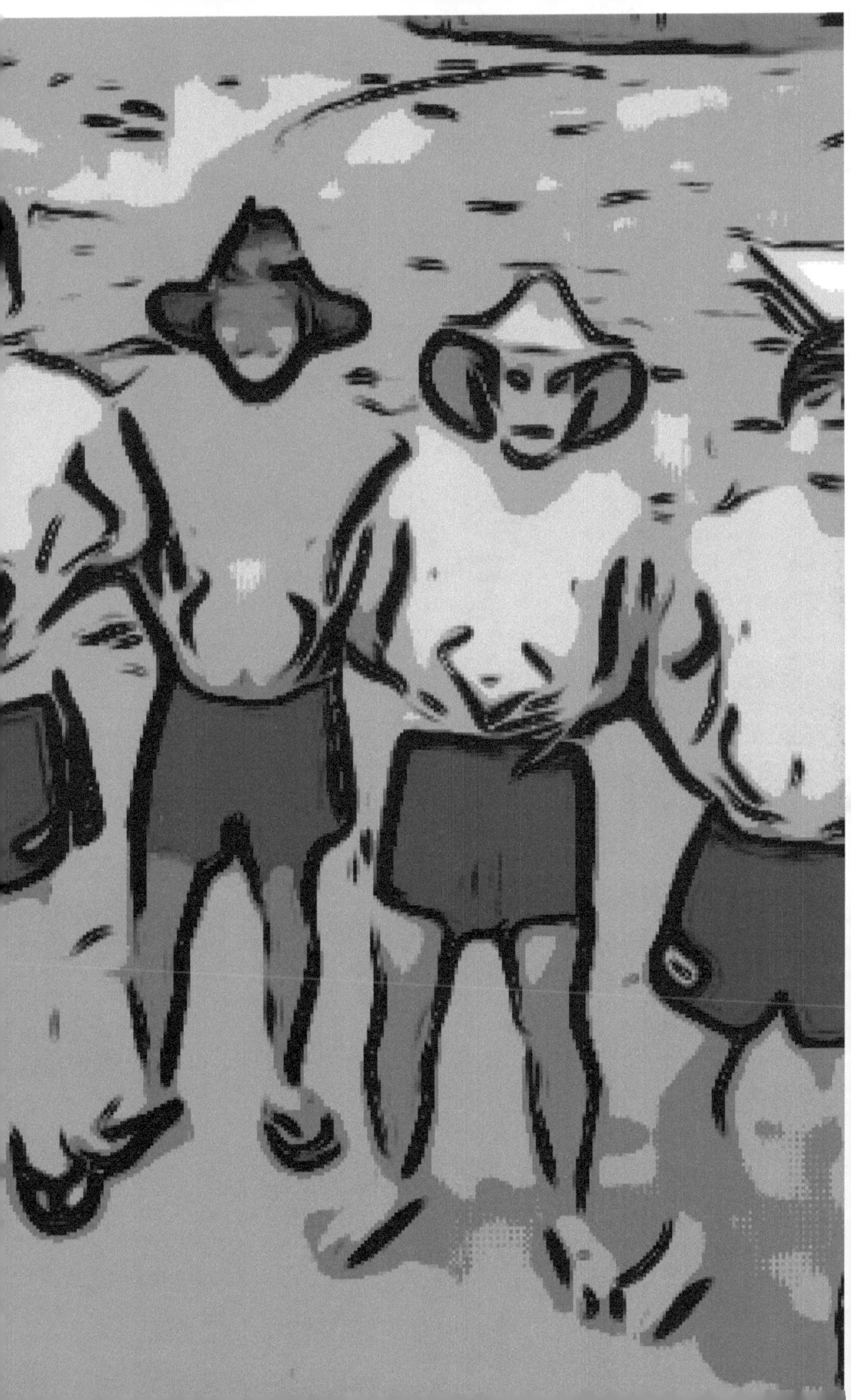

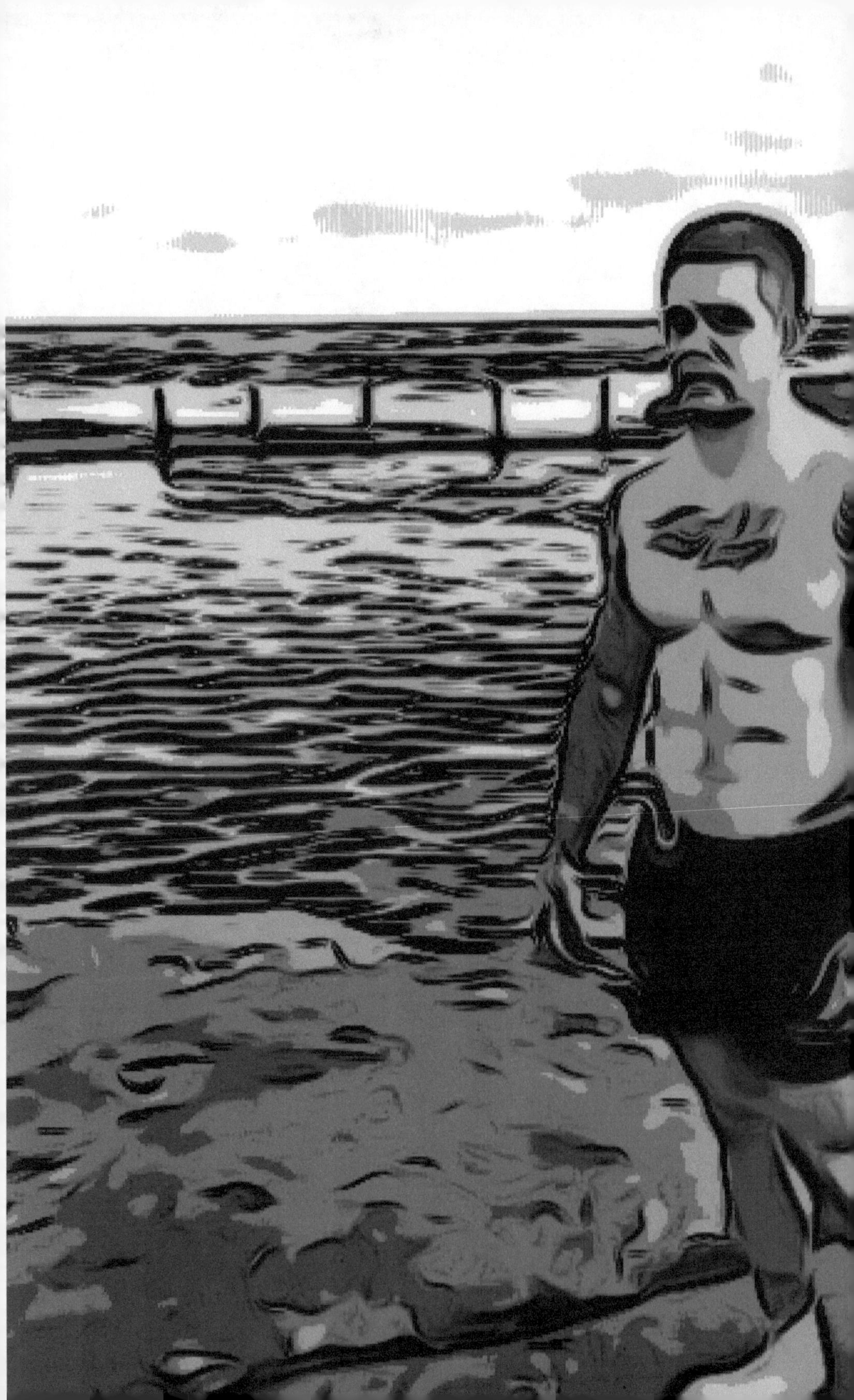

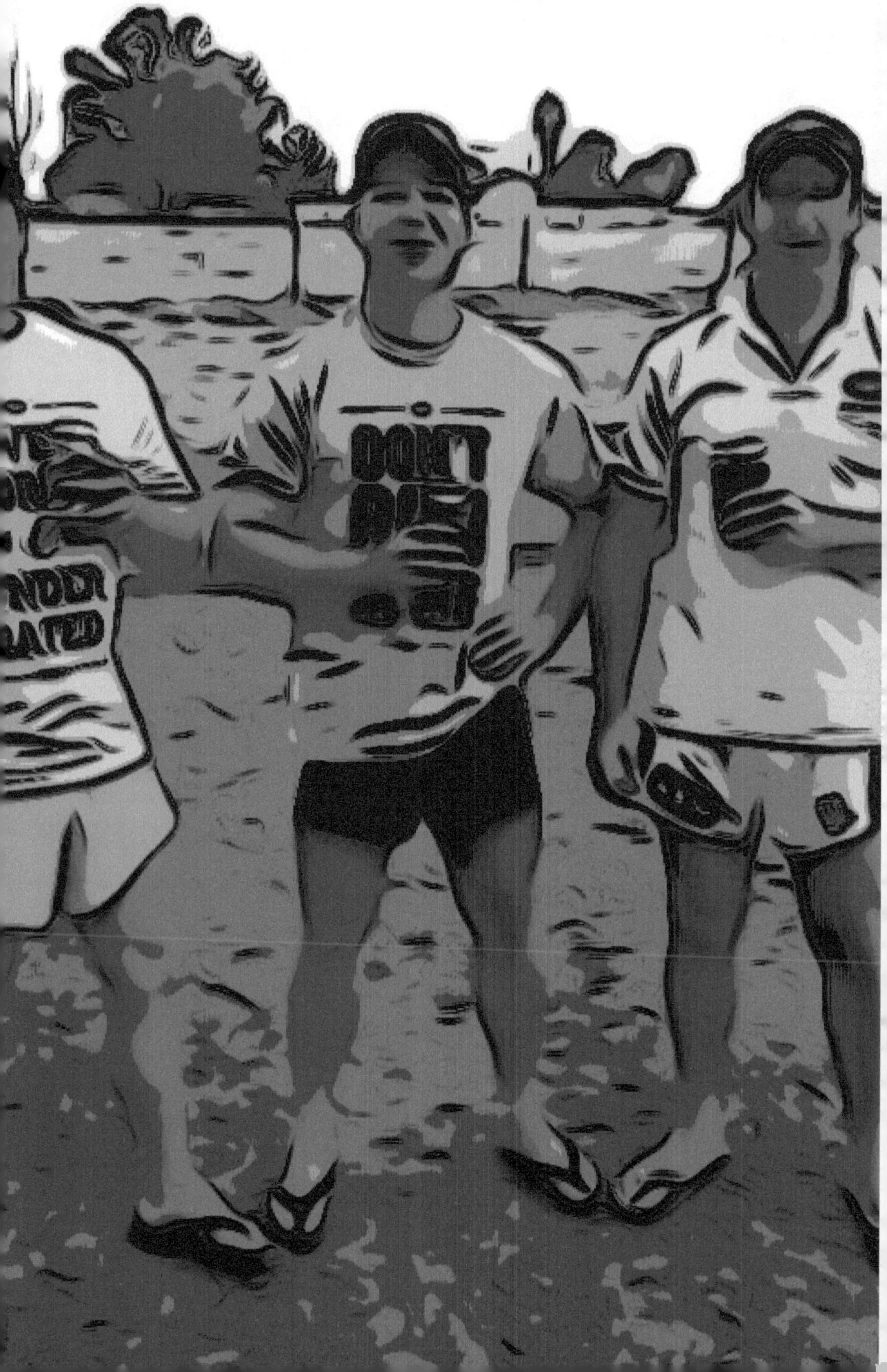
DON'T

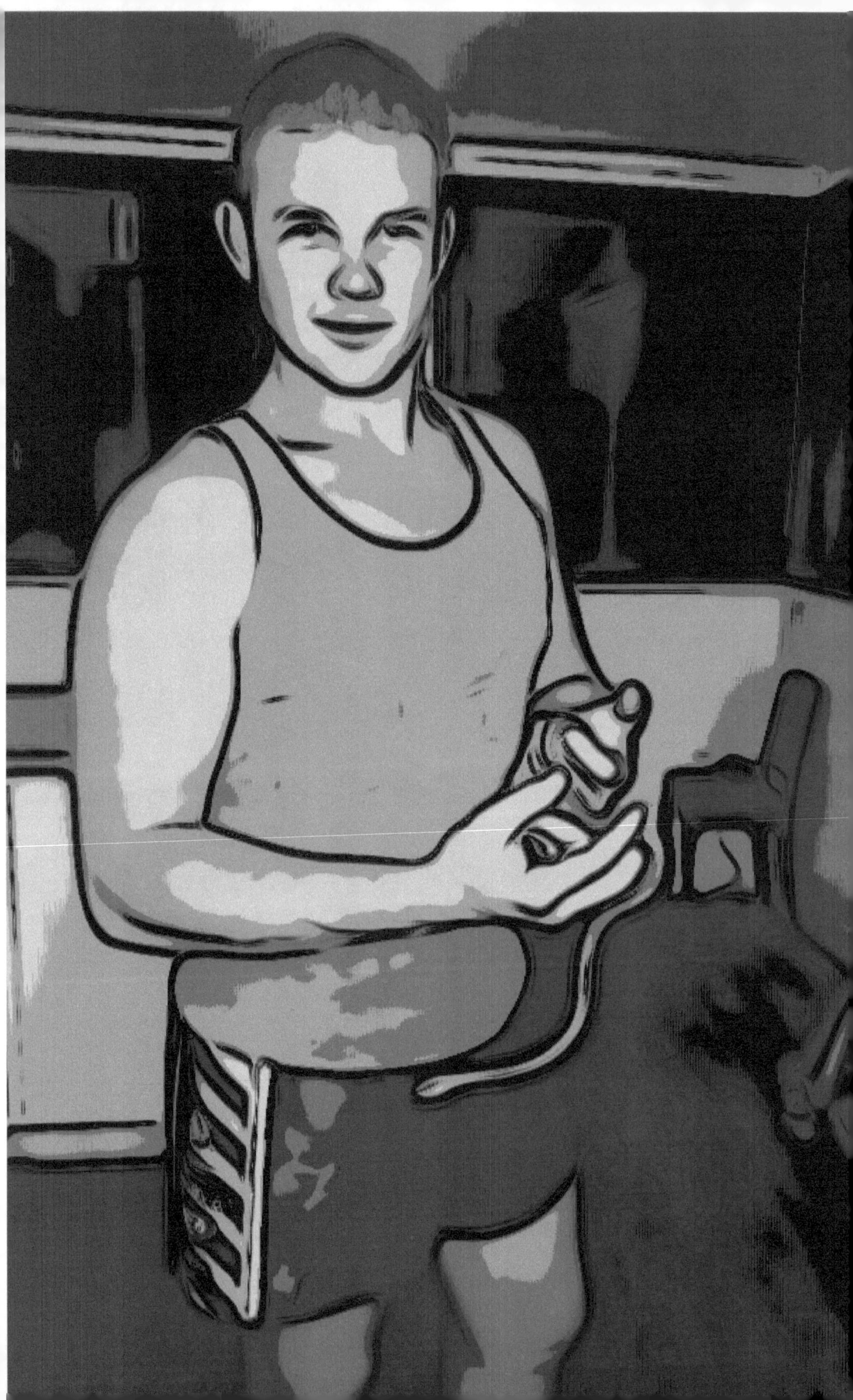

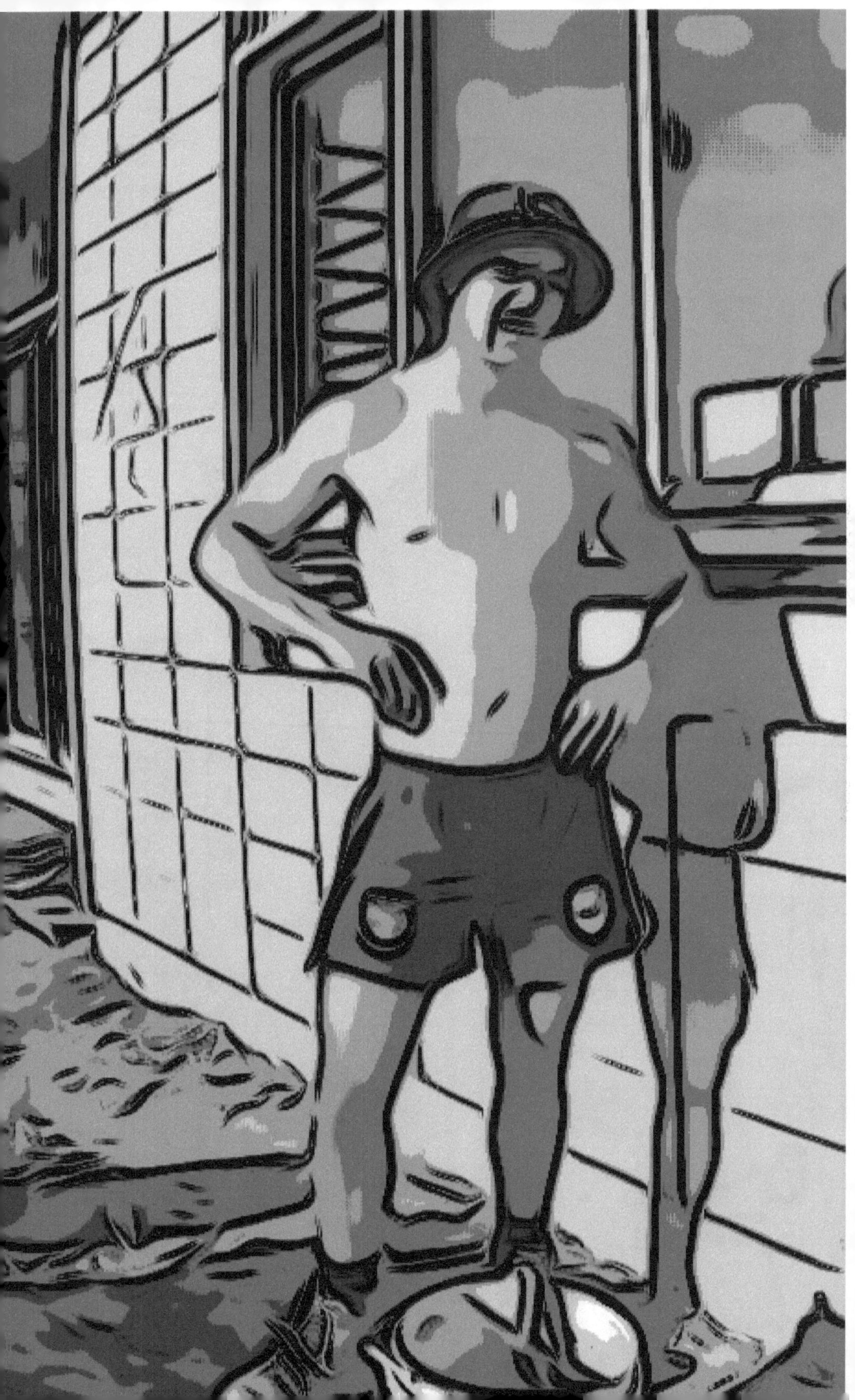

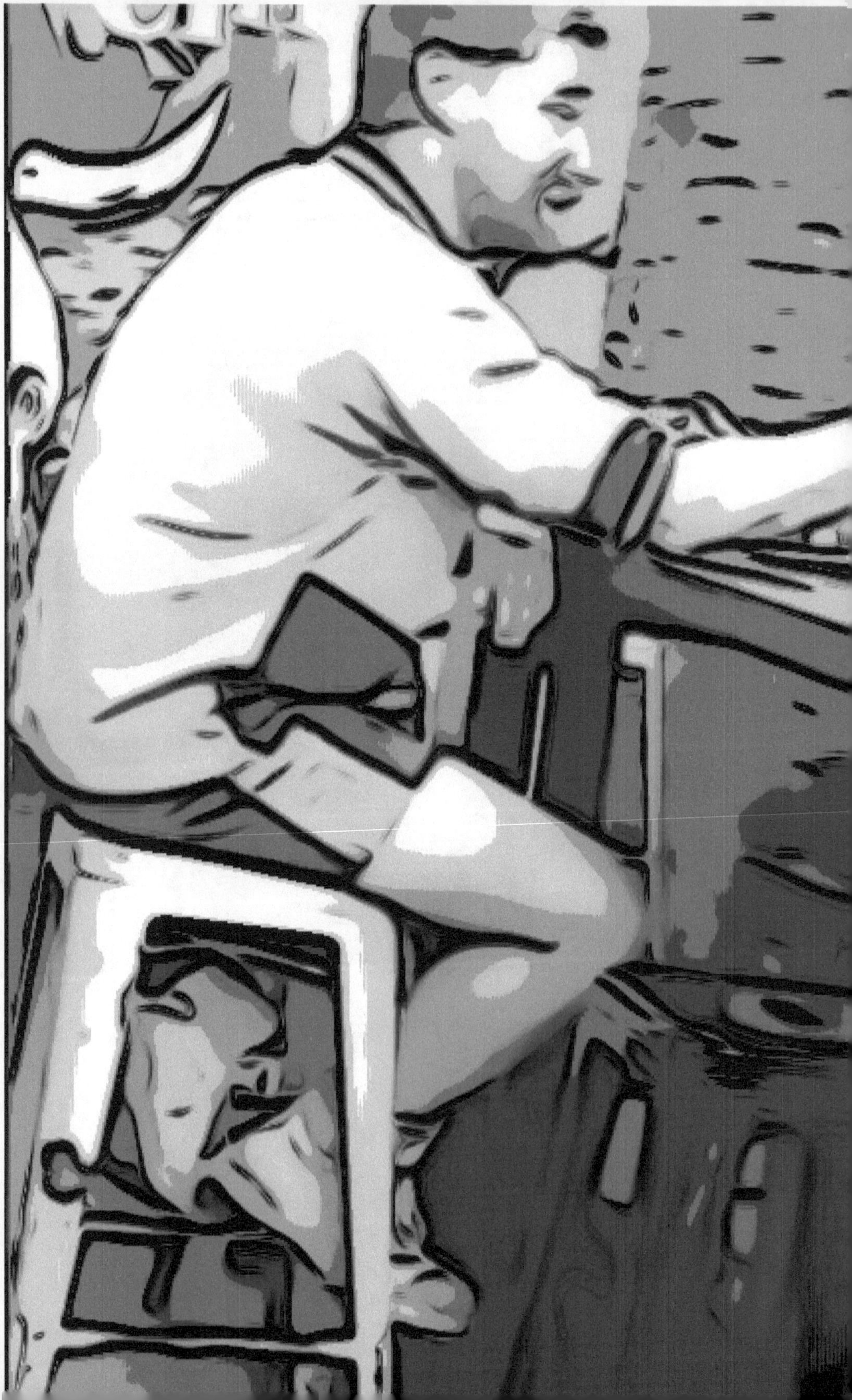

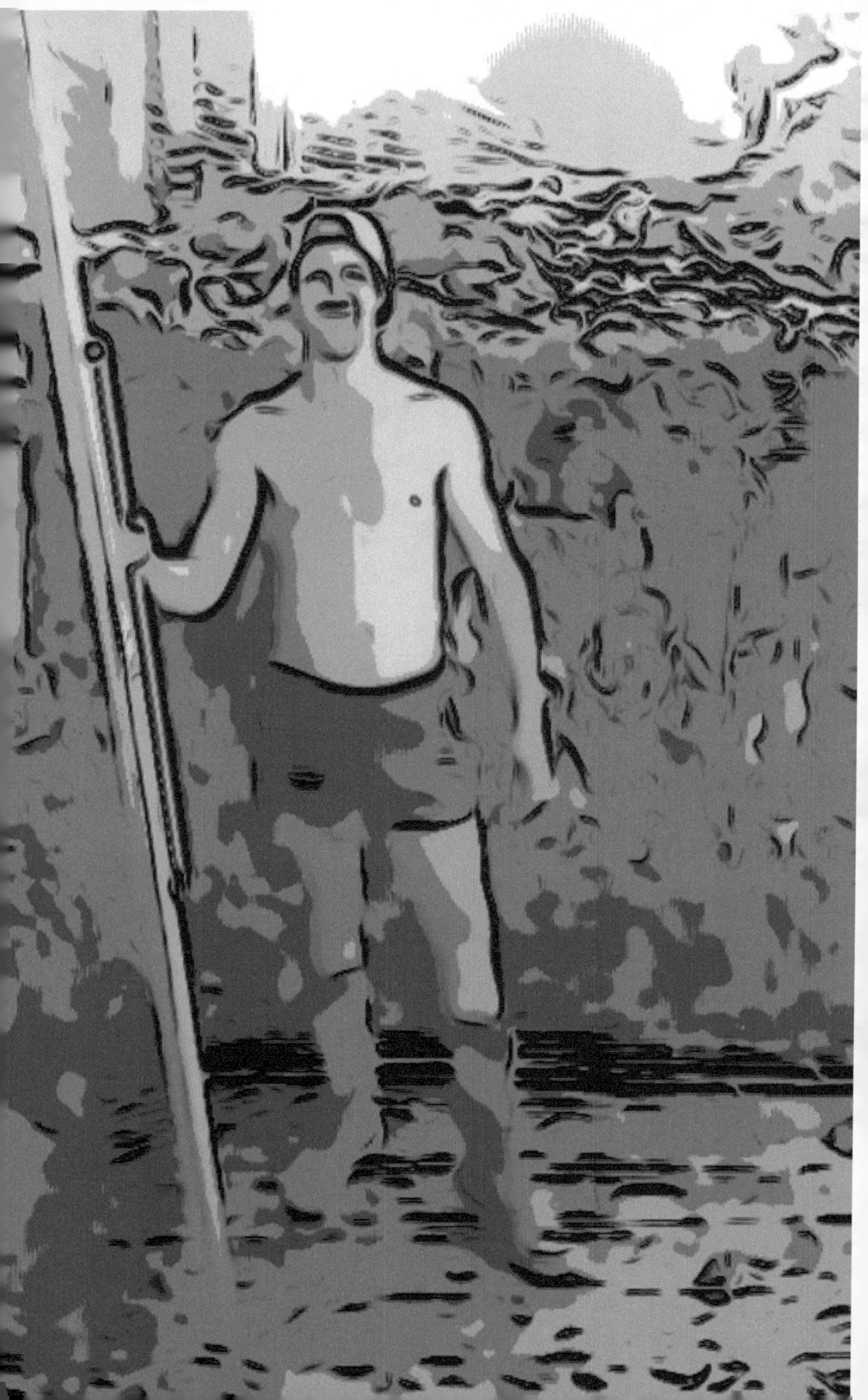

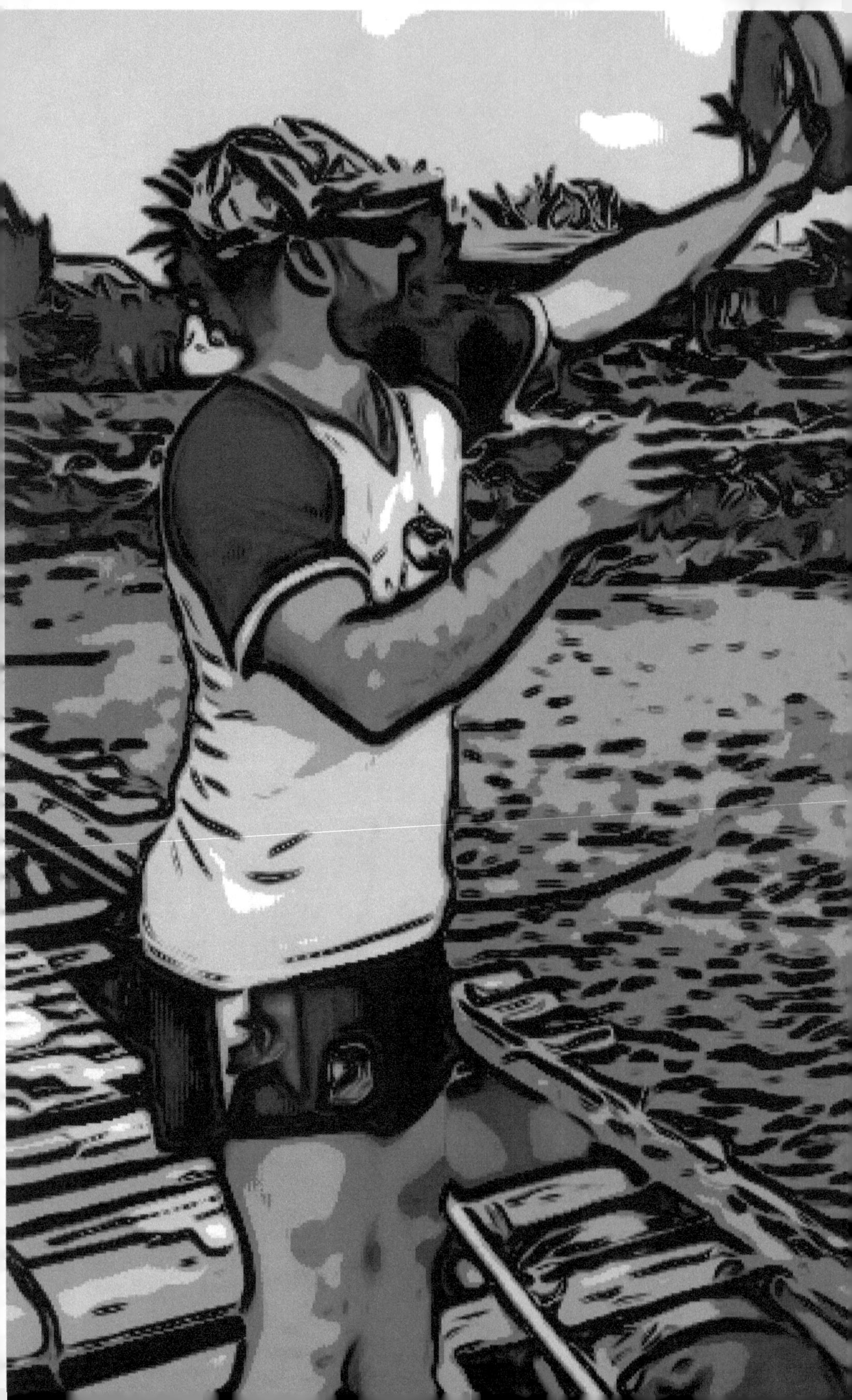

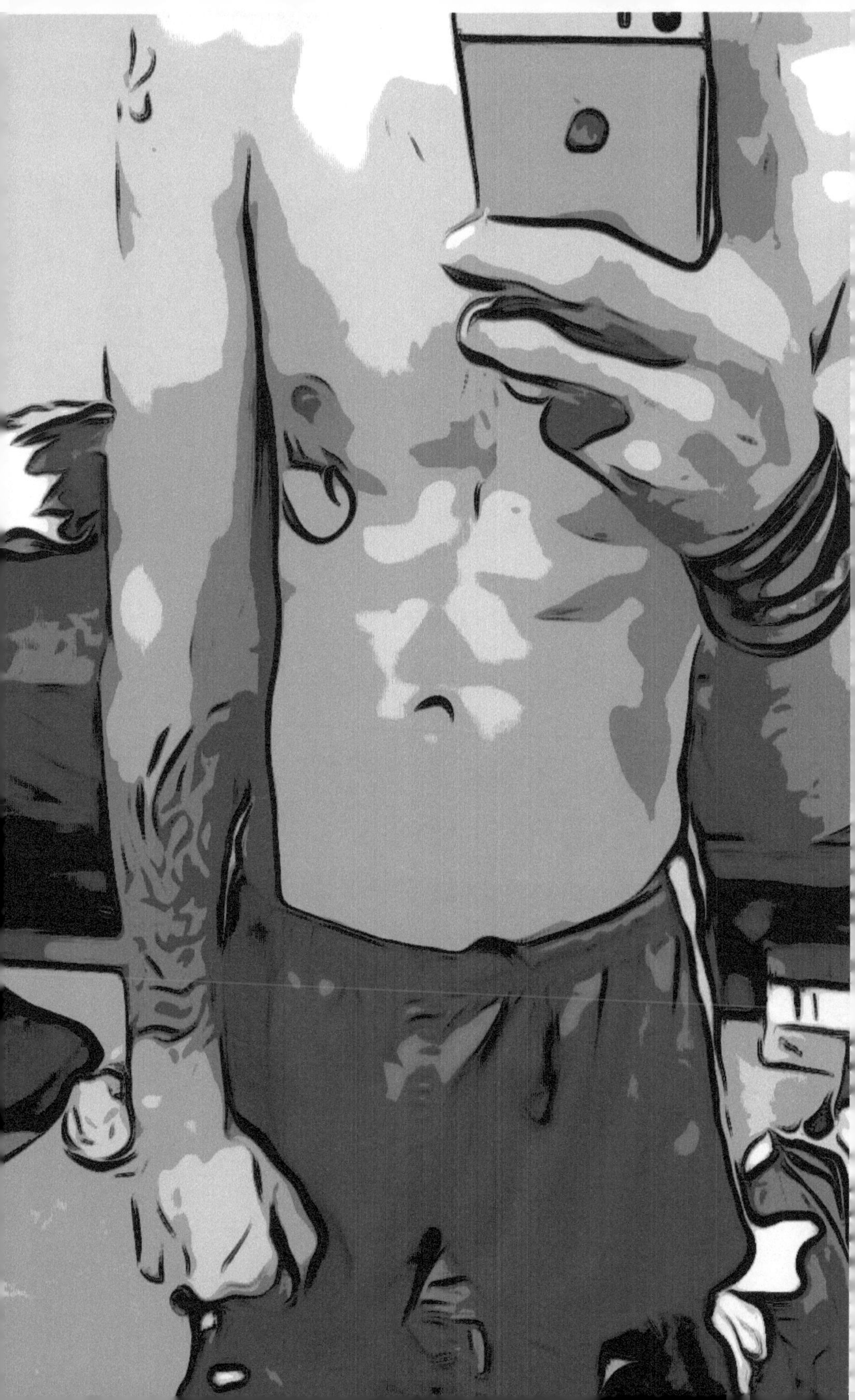

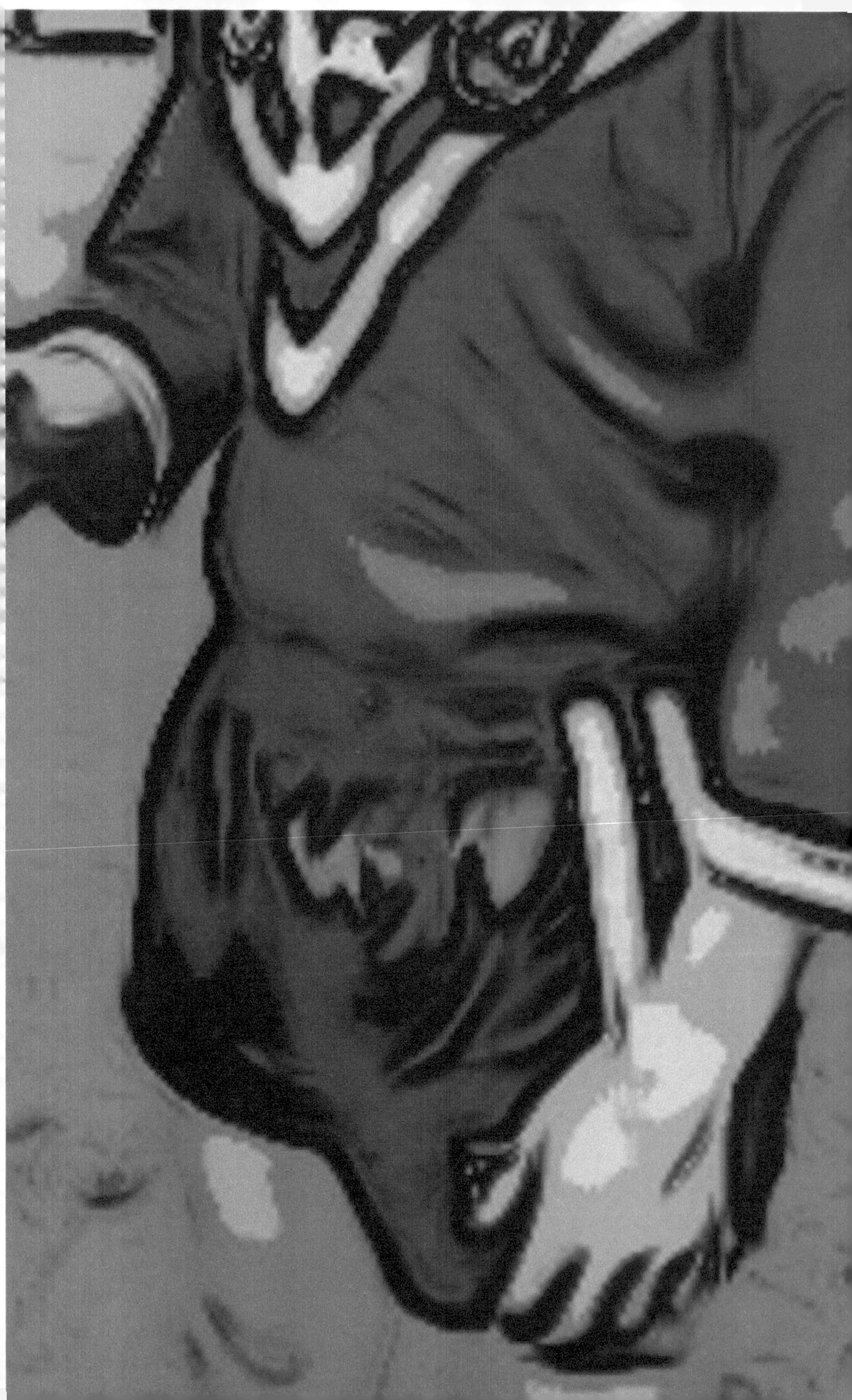

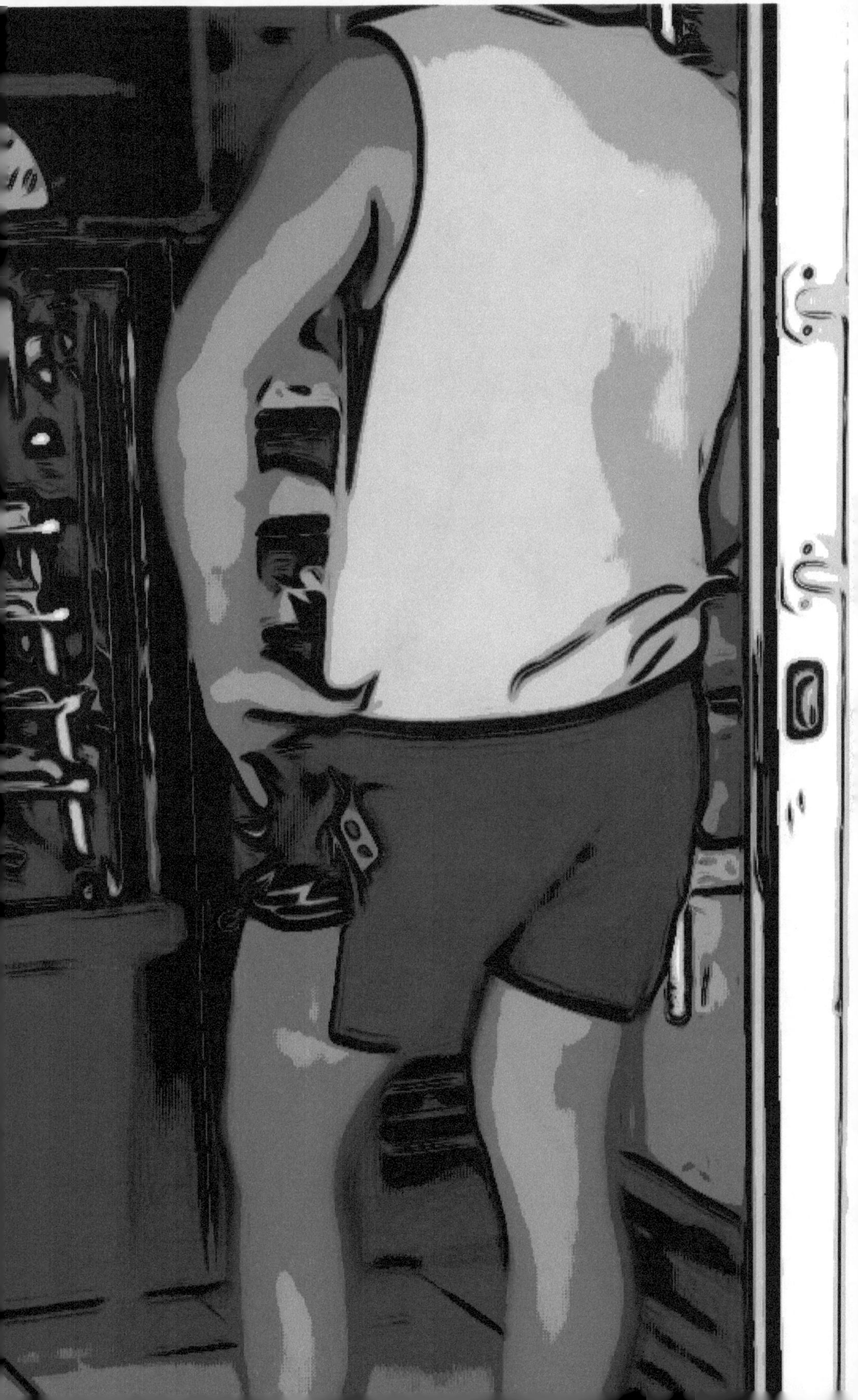

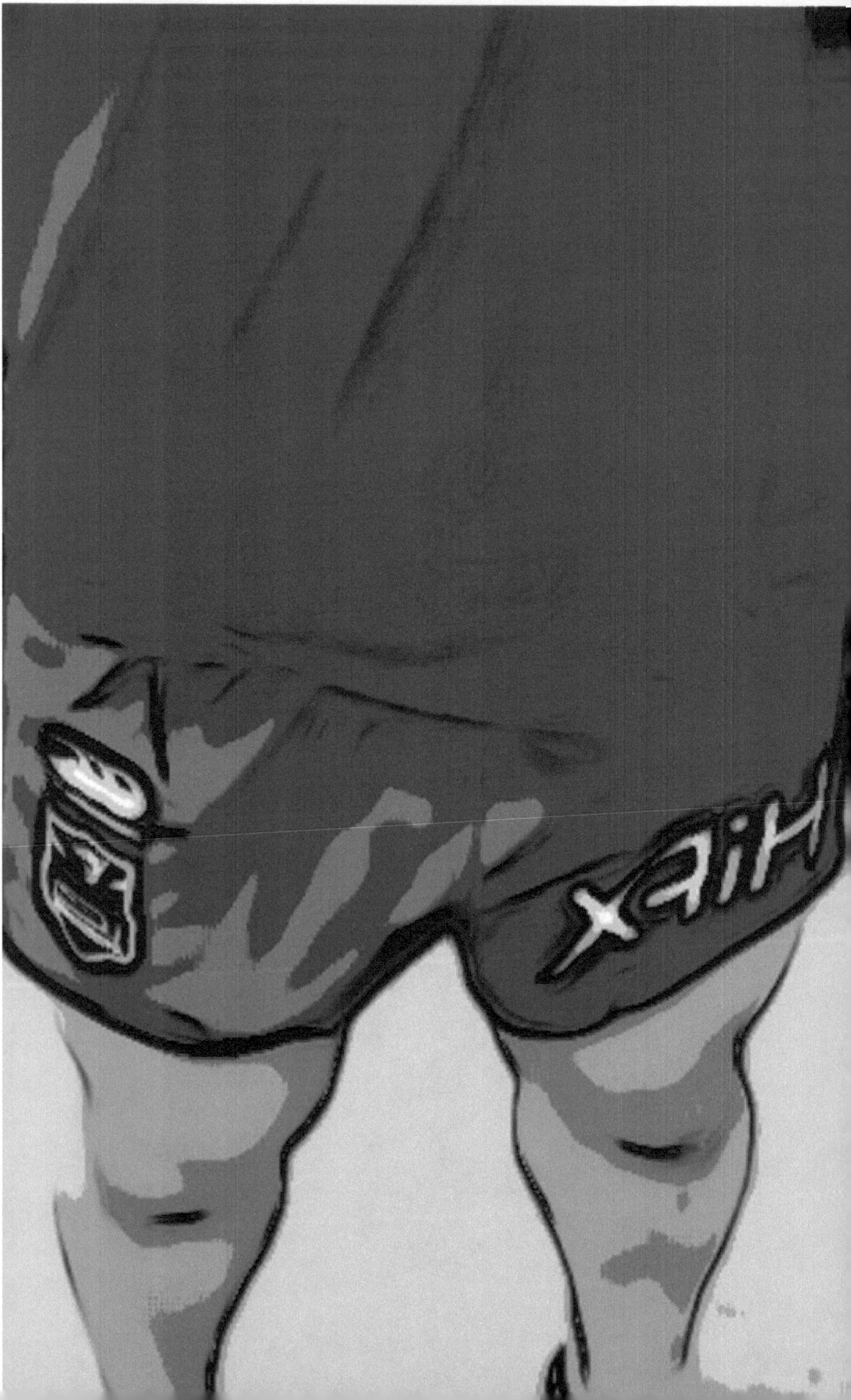

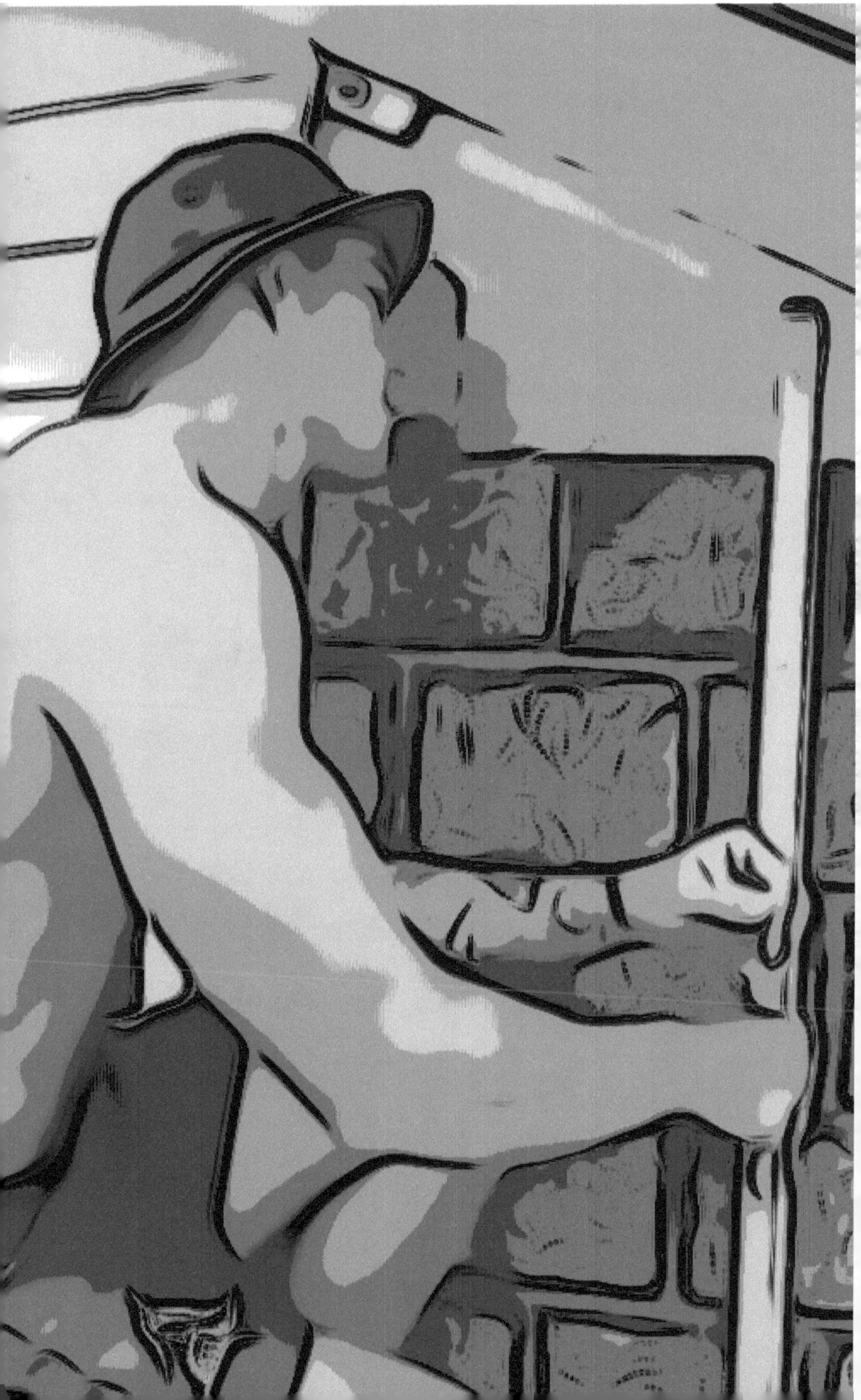

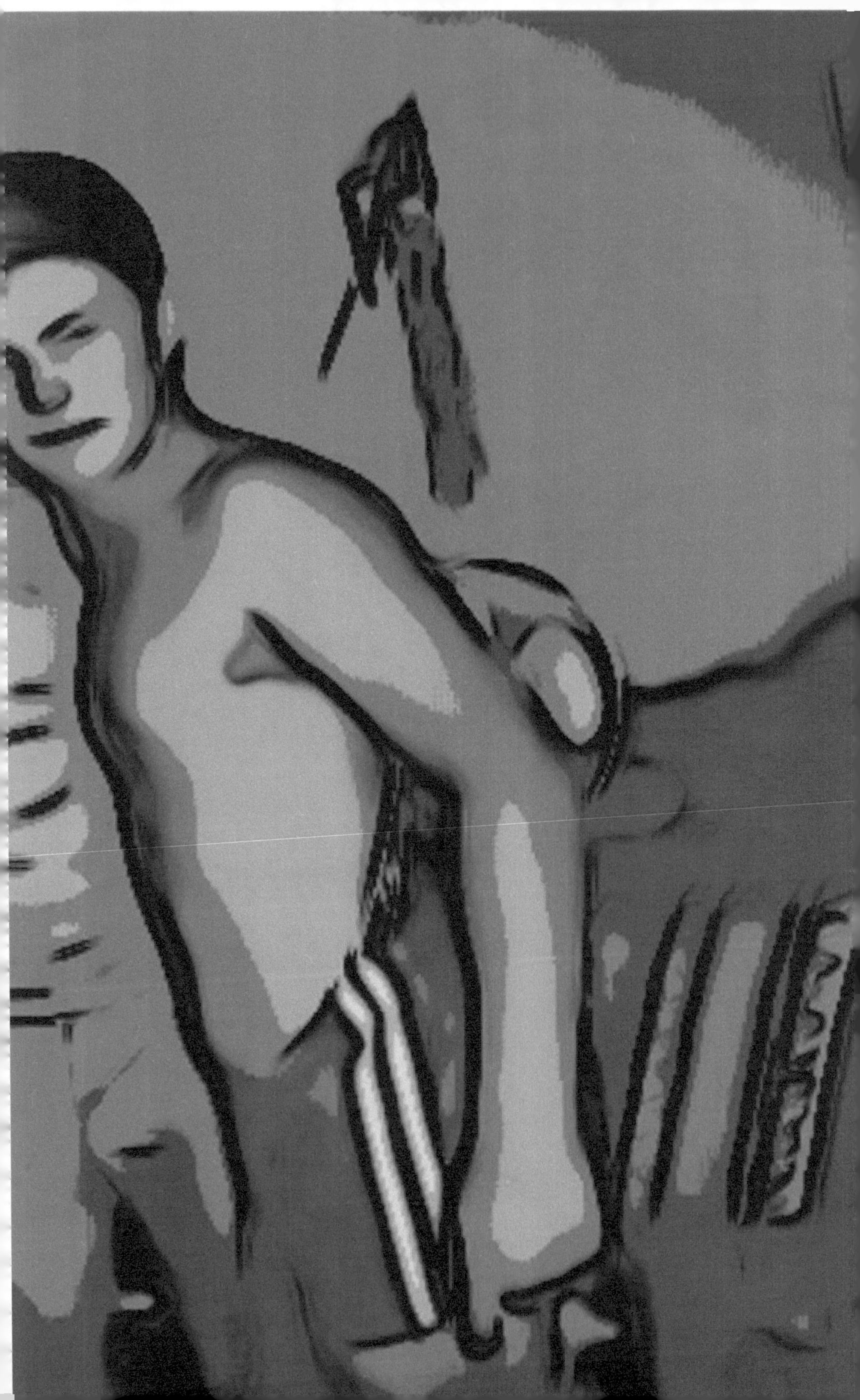

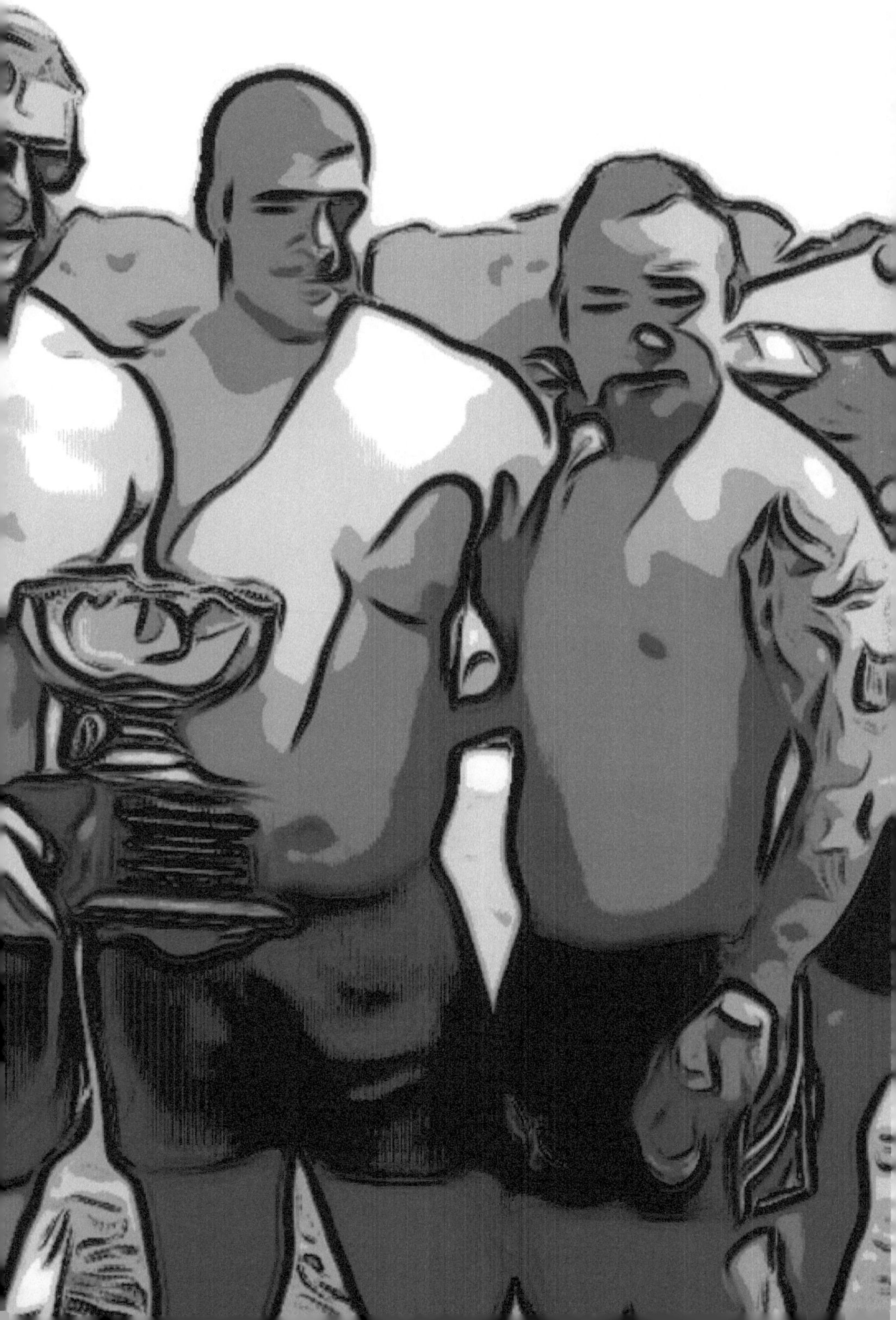

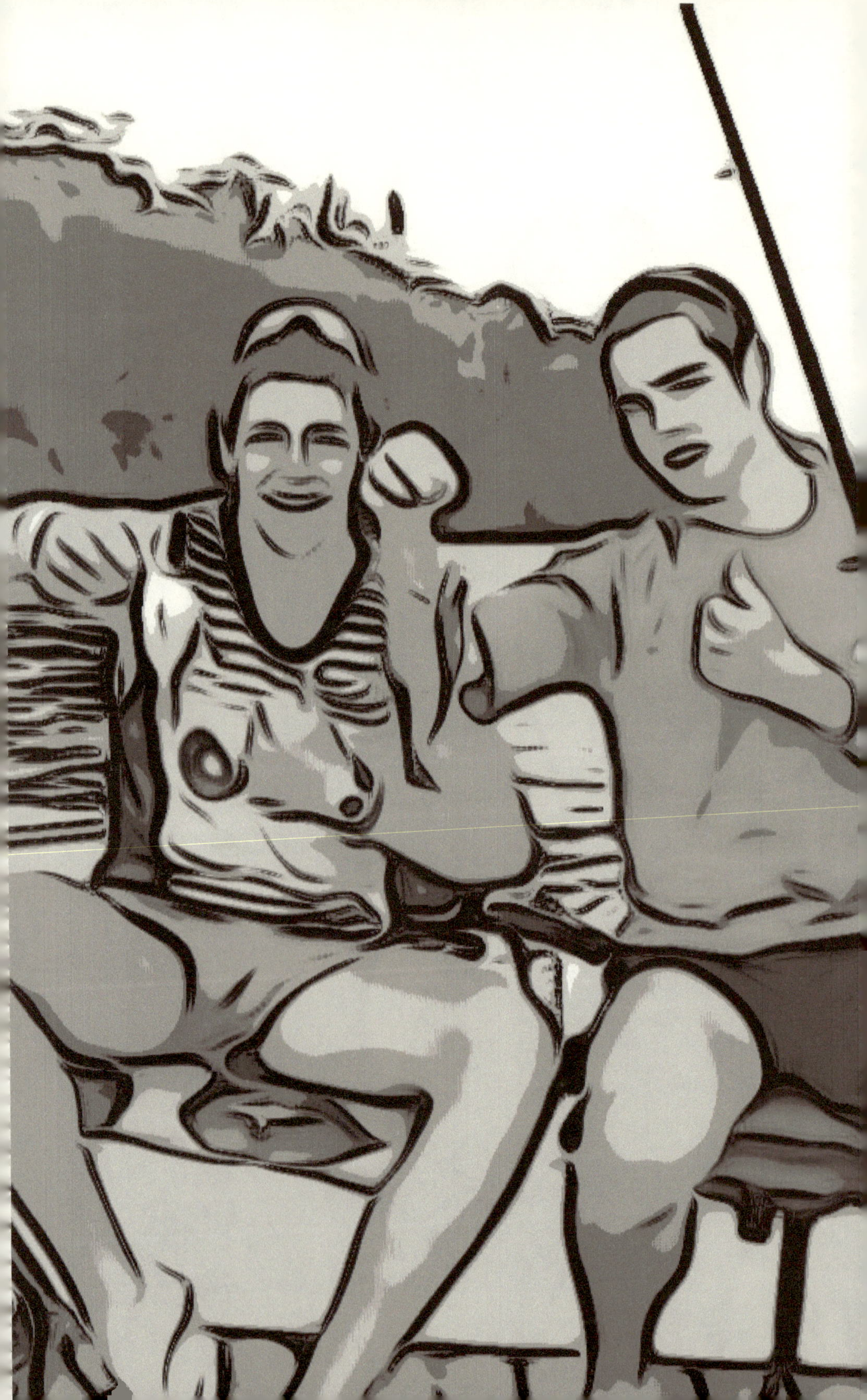

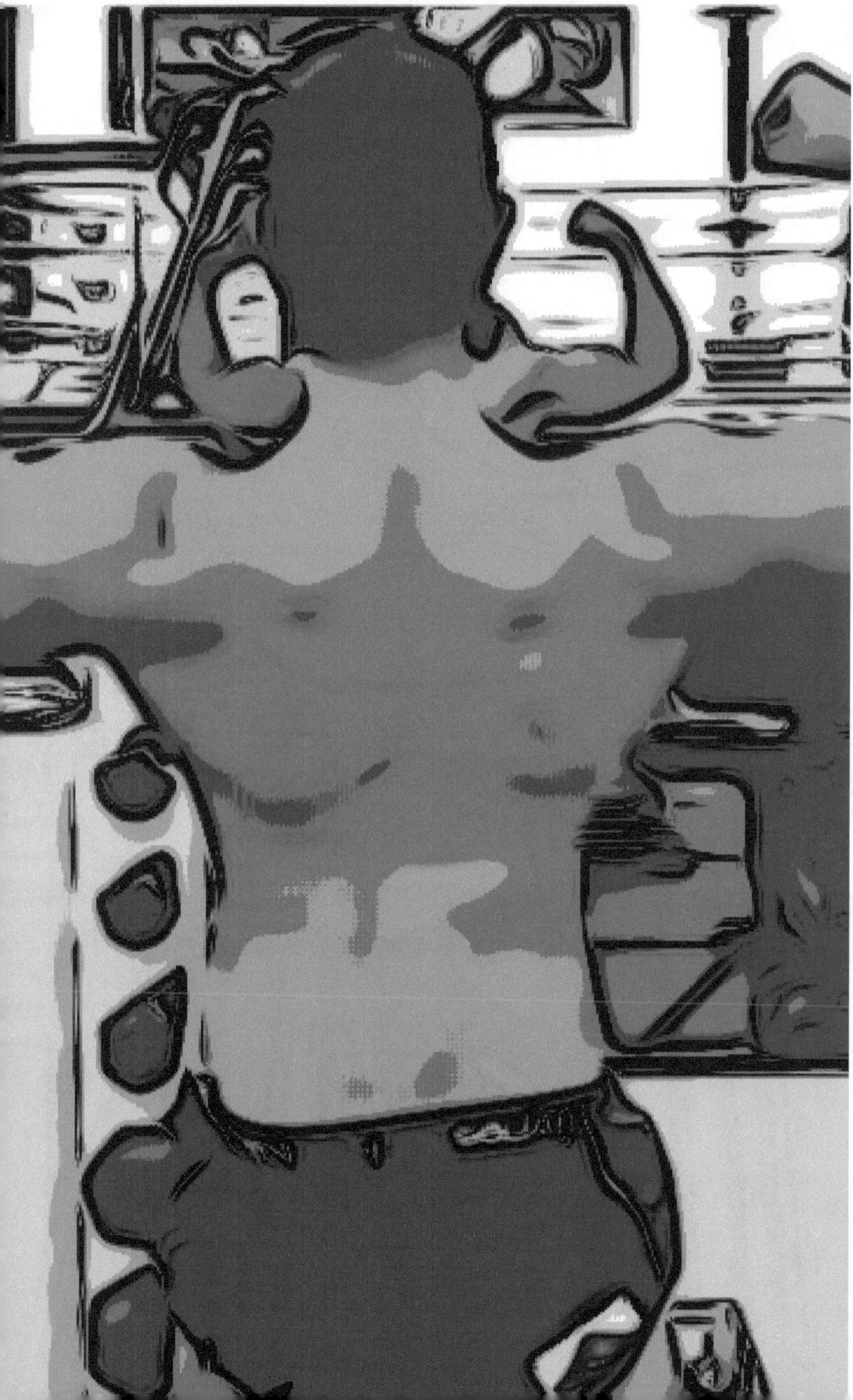

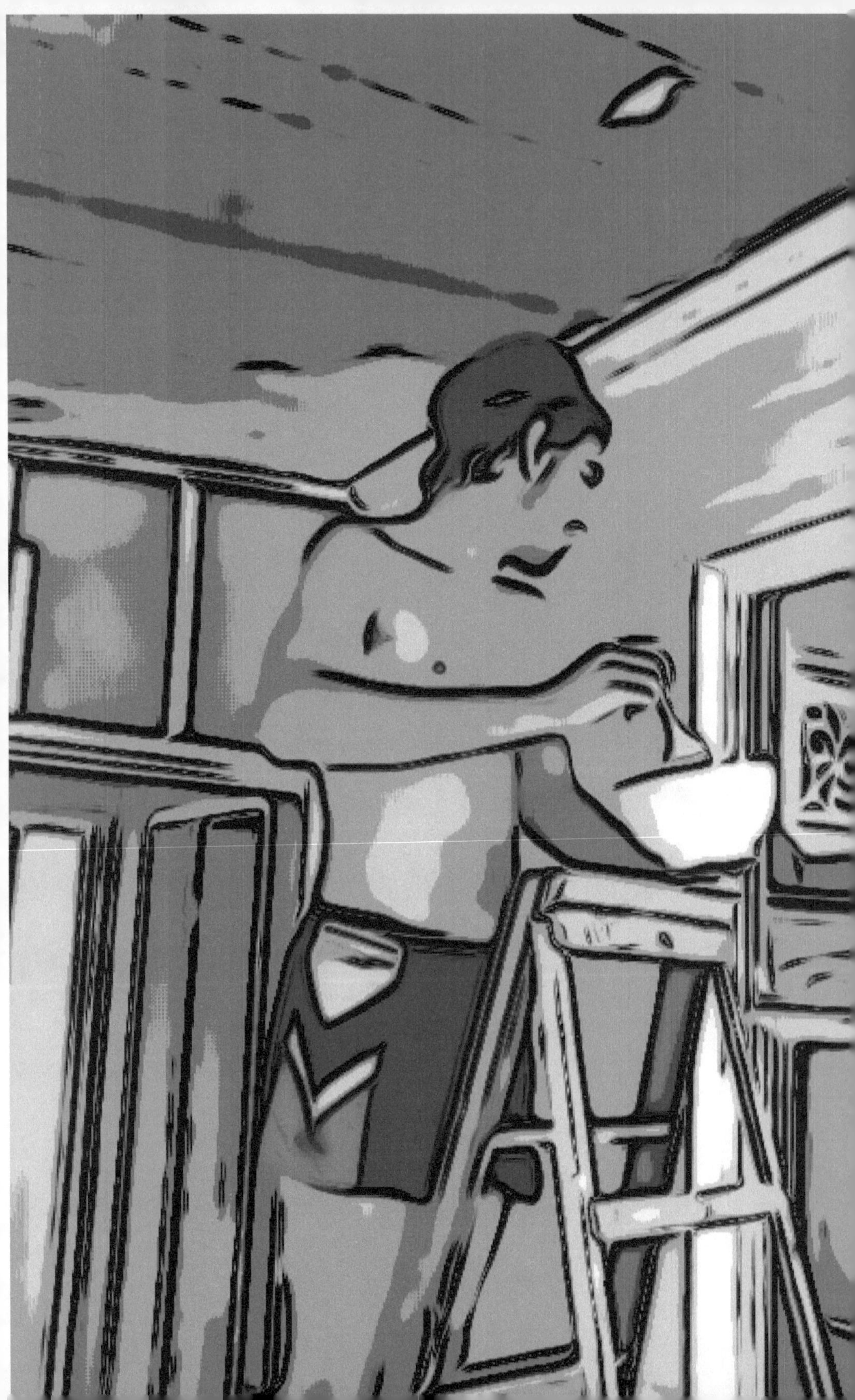

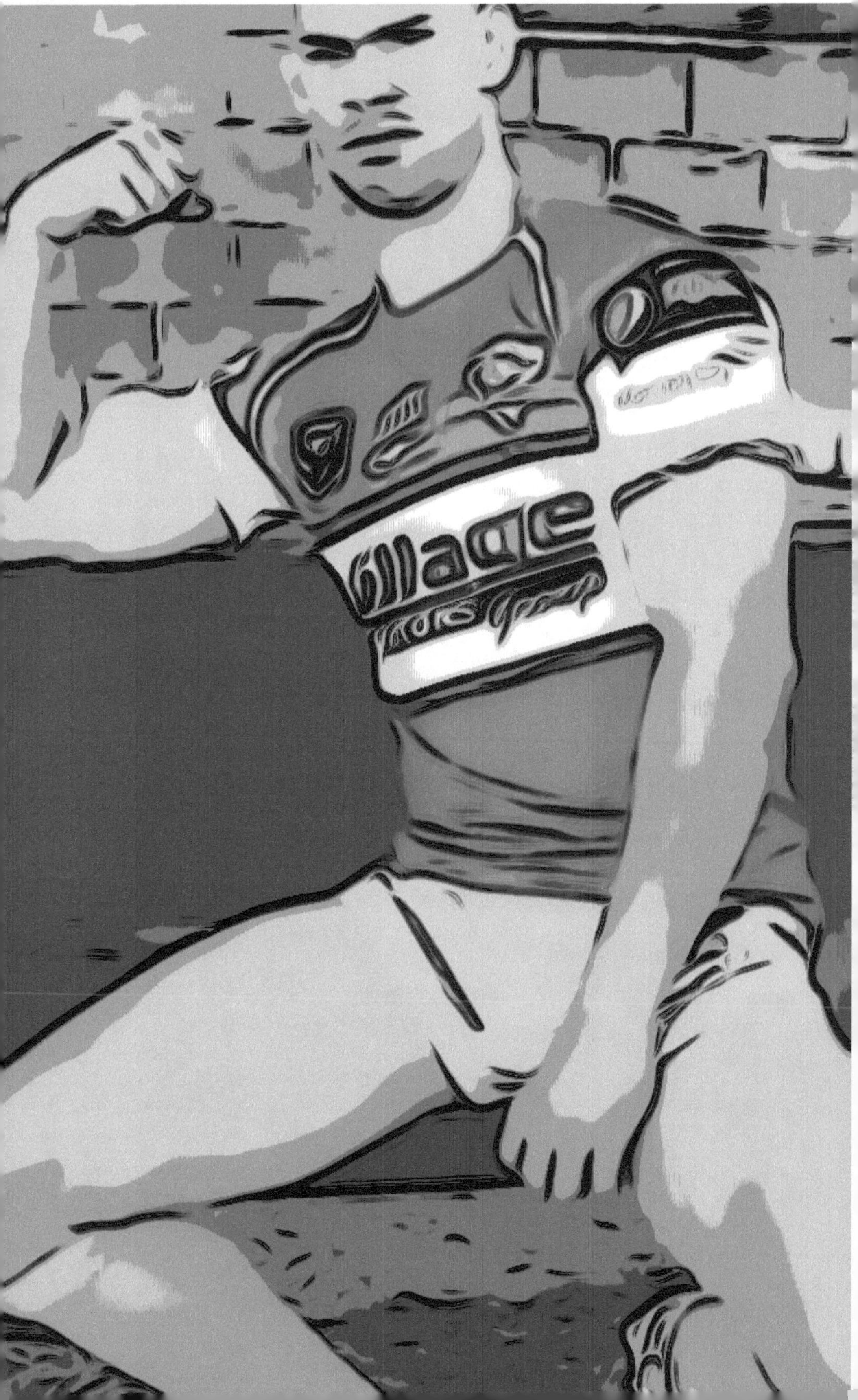

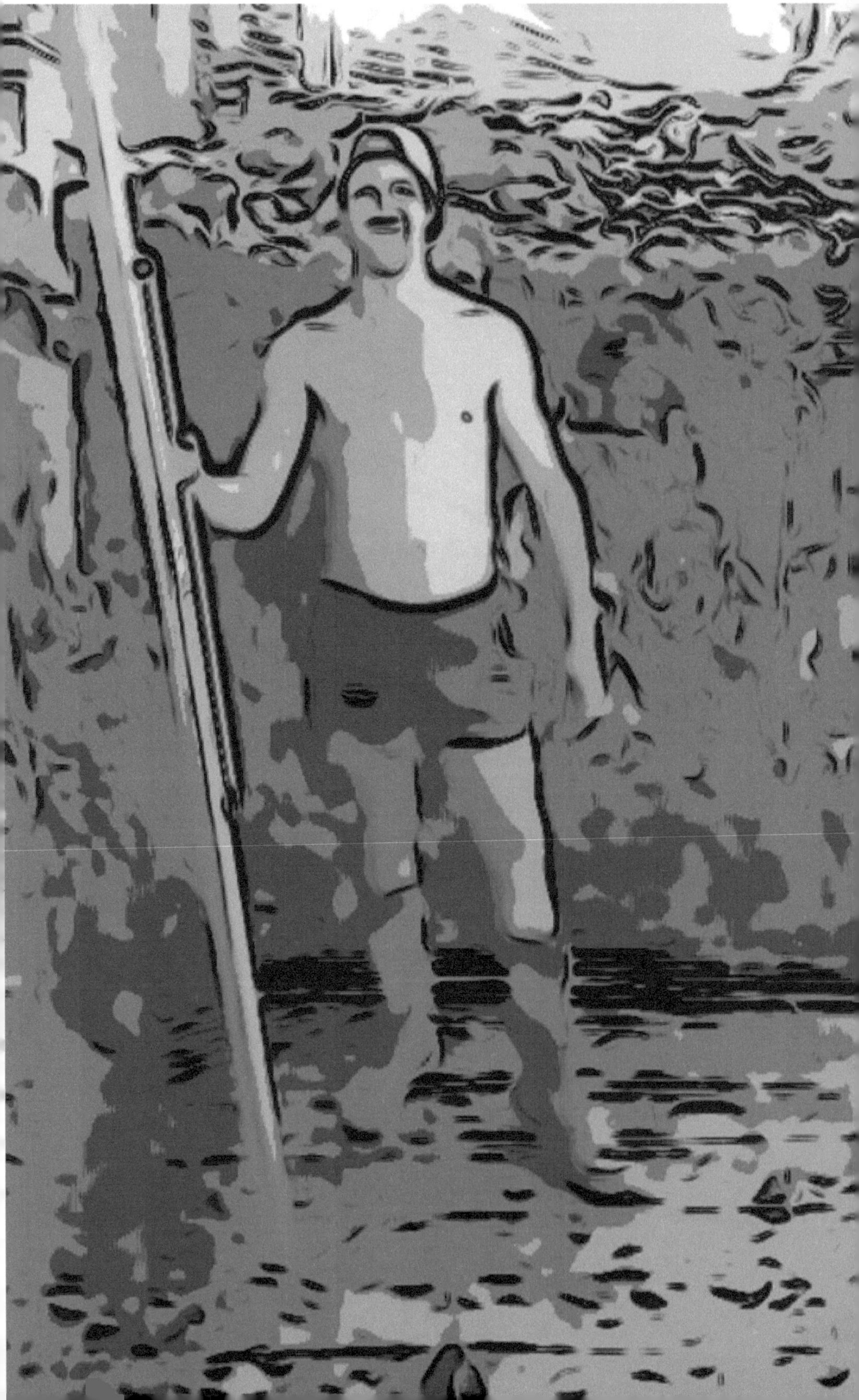

www.ingramcontent.com/pod-product-compliance
Lightning Source LLC
Chambersburg PA
CBHW030905180526
45163CB00004B/1719
* 9 7 8 0 3 5 9 9 8 2 7 9 0 *